D0510781

The Pope and the Beggar

Thoughts and Meditations with Pope Benedict XVI and Father Werenfried

Aid to the Church in Need

1

The Pope and the Beggar
Thoughts and Meditations with Pope Benedict XVI and Father Werenfried
© 2007 **Aid to the Church in Need**

Text edited by John Newton and Terry Murphy
Translations by Francis Davidson
Design by Terry Murphy

Published by
Aid to the Church in Need (UK)
12-14 Benhill Avenue
Sutton
SM1 4DA
Tel: 020 8642 8668   Email: acn@acnuk.org
Fax: 020 8661 6293   Website: www.acnuk.org
Registered with the Charity Commission No. 1097984

ISBN 978-0-9553339-3-4

Contents

Contents

Foreword

WHAT IS THE CONNECTION BETWEEN POPE Benedict XVI and Fr Werenfried? At first sight, the two seem to be contrasting characters: maybe Pope Benedict XVI has been seen as the intellectual theologian and Fr Werenfried – the late founder of Aid to the Church in Need – as the beggar for Christ. But both have challenged the assumptions and perspectives of this material world and called for people to turn to what is truly spiritual and eternal. I give you one example, as both the theologian and the beggar call us to live a Christ-centred life in today's world.

At the beginning of Lent 2007, the Holy Father challenged people to "de-tox" through fasting from sin and evil. He also said: "The Cross is for us men and women of our time – who all too often are distracted by earthly and momentary concerns and interests – the definitive revelation of divine love and mercy. God is love and his love is the secret of our happiness. However, to enter into this mystery of love there is no other way than that of losing ourselves, of giving ourselves to the way of the Cross."

Likewise, Fr Werenfried used to beg his benefactors to "return to the tradition of a fast linked with prayer and good works. All too often we deny the Cross that from age to age must redeem the world. The call to conversion is addressed to each one of us".

Long before he became Pope Benedict XVI, Cardinal Joseph Ratzinger was a friend and benefactor of Aid to the Church in Need. In June 2002 he described the charity as "a gift of Providence for our time" stating that ACN had "turned out to be one of the most important Catholic charities... It is working in a worthwhile manner all over the world. Our world is hungering and thirsting for witnesses of the risen Lord, for human beings who pass on the Faith in word and deed as well as for human beings who stand by those in need."

By publishing this book, Aid to the Church in Need is offering something to the Church in need *here* – that is, each and every one of us in the West. The thoughts and meditations which we have collected in this book explore a range of different themes to do with aspects of our daily Christian faith.

We hope and pray that these writings will help you in all that you face, and deepen your faith.

Thank you for your compassion and commitment to the suffering Church; you can be assured of the prayers of the communion of saints.

Neville Kyrke-Smith
National Director
Aid to the Church in Need UK

Creation

In the beginning
God created the heavens and the earth.
(Genesis 1.1 RSV)

The world does not exist by itself; it is brought into being by the creative Spirit of God, by the creative Word of God. For this reason Pentecost also mirrors God's wisdom. In its breadth and in the omni-comprehensive logic of its laws, God's wisdom permits us to glimpse something of his Creator Spirit. It elicits reverential awe.

Pope Benedict XVI
Meeting with the Ecclesial Movements
and New Communities, 3rd June 2006

Certainly, God has given a sign of himself in the greatness and power of the cosmos, from which we may dimly perceive something of the power of the Creator. But the real sign that he chose is hiddenness, from the wretched people of Israel to the Child at Bethlehem to the man who died on the cross with the words: "My God, my God, why have you forsaken me?" (Mt 27.46) This sign of hiddenness points us towards the fact that the reality of truth and love, the actual reality of God, is not to be met within the world of quantities but can be found only if we rise above that into a new order.

Pope Benedict XVI
What it means to be a Christian, p. 38

God's hand caresses the earth. His gentle countenance is bent with care over its wounds. The eternal Bearer and Restorer of things walks through its desecrated paradise to draw good from human evil.

Fr. Werenfried van Straaten

11

God is everywhere, and yet there are various stages in his proximity, because each higher level of being is a little closer to him. But wherever understanding and love grow, we reach a new kind of closeness, a new form of his presence.

Joseph Cardinal Ratzinger
God and the World, p. 107

Those very people who, as Christians, believe in the Creator Spirit become aware of the fact that we cannot use and abuse the world and matter merely as material for our actions and desires; that we must consider creation a gift that has not been given to us to be destroyed, but to become God's garden, hence, a garden for men and women.

Pope Benedict XVI
Meeting with the Ecclesial Movements
and New Communities, 3rd June 2006

In the face of the many forms of abuse of the earth that we see today, let us listen, as it were, to the groaning of creation of which St Paul speaks (Rom 8.22); let us begin by understanding the Apostle's words, that creation waits with impatience for the revelation that we are children of God, to be set free from bondage and obtain his splendour.

Pope Benedict XVI
Meeting with the Ecclesial Movements
and New Communities, 3rd June 2006

Nature can be marvellous. The starry heaven is stupendous. But my reaction to that remains no more than an impersonal wonder, because that, in the end, means that I am myself no more than a tiny part of an enormous machine. The real God, however, is more than that. He is not just nature, but the One who came before it and who sustains it: and the whole of God, so faith tells us, is the act of relating. That is what we mean when we say that he is a Trinity, that is threefold. Because he is in himself a complex of relationships, he can also make other beings who are grounded in relationships and who may relate to him, because he has related them to himself.

Joseph Cardinal Ratzinger
God and the World, p. 97

We must make God present again in our society. This seems to me to be the first essential element: that God be once again present in our lives, that we do not live as though we were autonomous, authorised to invent what freedom and life are. We must realize that we are creatures, aware that there is a God who has created us and that living in accordance with his will is not dependence but a gift of love that makes us alive.

Pope Benedict XVI
Meeting with the young people of
the diocese of Rome, 6th April 2006

God renews the face of the earth. He stands as a physician at humanity's bed of suffering. The misshapen work of unknowing creatures he covers with glory. Where his shining fingers lovingly caress, creation lies softly glowing.

Fr. Werenfried van Straaten

Light

For with thee is the fountain of life;
in thy light do we see light.
(Psalm 36.9 RSV)

Something of the light of God shines through the great religions of the world, of course, and yet they remain a matter of fragments and questions. But if the question about God finds no answer, if the road to him is blocked, if there is no forgiveness, which can only come with the authority of God himself, then human life is nothing but a meaningless experiment. Thus, God himself has parted the clouds at a certain point. He has turned on the light and has shown us the way that it is the truth, that makes it possible for us to live, and that is life itself.

Joseph Cardinal Ratzinger
God and the World, p. 323

We are living in alienation, in the salt waters of suffering and death; in a sea of darkness without light. The net of the Gospel pulls us out of the waters of death and brings us into the splendour of God's light, into true life.

Pope Benedict XVI
Address to mark the official beginning
of his pontificate, 24th April 2005

As the Lord came from the Father and has given us light, life and love, so too our mission must continually set us in motion – make us restless – to bring the joy of Christ to those who suffer, those who doubt, and also those who mourn.

Pope Benedict XVI
Priestly ordination in St Peter's,
15th May 2005

Sometimes we even feel like saying to God, If you had only made man a little less great, then he would be less dangerous. If you hadn't given him his freedom, then he would not be able to fall so far. And yet, we don't quite dare to say it in the end, because at the same time we are grateful that God did put greatness into man. And if he takes upon himself the risk inherent in man's freedom and all the falls from greatness it involves, then we feel horrified by the thought of what that might mean, and we have to try to summon up all the positive forces at our command, but we also have to share in God's fundamental attitude of putting trust in man. And only by holding fast to this fundamental trust are we able to set ourselves to oppose the dangers that threaten man and to find them bearable.

Joseph Cardinal Ratzinger
God and the World, p. 323

We want to be a Church open to the future, rich in promises for the new generations. It is not a matter of pandering to youth, which is basically ridiculous, but of a true youthfulness that flows from the wellsprings of eternity, that is ever new, that derives from the transparency of Christ in his Church: this is how he gives us the light to continue.

Pope Benedict XVI
Meeting with the German bishops in Cologne,
World Youth Day, 21st August 2005

The Church must manifest the full beauty of Christ, like the lamp on a lamp stand and the city on the mountain-top, instead of conforming herself to the world. For only then, at this crucial turning point in world history, will she be in a position to pass on to those who come after us the spiritual treasures that have been entrusted to her.

Fr. Werenfried van Straaten

Through all the ups and downs of history, [the Saints] were the true reformers who constantly rescued it from plunging into the valley of darkness; it was they who constantly shed upon it the light that was needed to make sense – even in the midst of suffering – of God's words spoken at the end of the work of creation: "It is very good".

Pope Benedict XVI
Homily at the vigil with the young people,
World Youth Day, Cologne, 24ᵗʰ August 2005

We want to be a Church open to the future, rich in promises for the new generations. It is not a matter of pandering to youth, which is basically ridiculous, but of a true youthfulness that flows from the wellsprings of eternity, that is ever new, that derives from the transparency of Christ in his Church: this is how he gives us the light to continue.

Pope Benedict XVI
Meeting with the German bishops in Cologne,
World Youth Day, 21ˢᵗ August 2005

It is growing dark on earth. When will the John arise, to bear witness again to the light? And when will the Word again become flesh in us so that the nations in the grip of fear may see his glory, the glory as of the only begotten Son of the Father, full of grace and truth?

Fr. Werenfried van Straaten

The relics of the Saints are traces of that invisible but real presence which sheds light upon the shadows of the world and reveals the Kingdom of Heaven in our midst. They cry out with us and for us: "Maranatha!" – "Come, Lord Jesus!"

Pope Benedict XVI
Papal welcoming ceremony on the banks of the Rhine,
World Youth Day, Cologne, 18th August 2005

Christmas

And the Word became flesh
and dwelt among us,
full of grace and truth;
we have beheld his glory,
glory as of the only Son from the Father.
(John 1.14 RSV)

Christmas is the feast of the great yearning for our better selves, for the pure and upright child in each of us, for the heaven we seek in vain on earth and for the peace we will only find in heaven...

Fr. Werenfried van Straaten

Jesus assumed our flesh; let us give him our own. In this way he can come into the world and transform it.

Pope Benedict XVI
Chrism Mass, Holy Thursday
in St Peter's, Rome, 13th April 2006

As Christmas draws near, the brilliance of the Christmas tree and the old carols ringing out around the crib or on the radio will remind you of the unforgettable story of Mary and Joseph, journeying because of an emperor's whim through the difficult mountain country to Bethlehem, where there was no room for them at the inn. Thus began the story of our salvation.

Fr. Werenfried van Straaten

The Christian faith brings us exactly that consolation, that God is so great that he can become small. And that is actually for me the unexpected and preciously inconceivable greatness of God, that he can later put him aside and put on another garment, but that he becomes that man.

Joseph Cardinal Ratzinger
God and the World, p. 31

Our salvation was dearly bought, not only on Calvary but also in Bethlehem. The song of the angels, the goodness of the shepherds and the faith of the wise men should never cause us to forget the tragedy that comes down to us in the Christmas story. The tragedy of closed doors and hearts. The scandal of loveless inhospitality and of the stable in which the Lord was born. The hatred of Herod, who saw a political danger in the defenceless baby. The fear of Mary and Joseph – forced to flee suddenly, head over heels into the street, to the frontier late in the night, fleeing breathlessly from one hiding place to another while behind them the shrieks of the dying children and the despairing screams of their mothers rose to heaven.

Fr. Werenfried van Straaten

Christmas is more than a family festival with a Christmas tree, candlelight, tinsel and roast turkey on the table. It is Christ's coming into a cold, dark, unredeemed world. Certainly at Christmas you may celebrate the incarnation of God with all the joy of redeemed man. There can be no objection to preparing a festive meal. But you must not forget what is essential: that Christ wants to become man again in his holy Church and in each one of us, so that in us his form, his goodness, his mercy, his love of men and his helpfulness may shine out in the darkness of this age.

Fr. Werenfried van Straaten

On Christmas night I took you all with me to the manger and laid the prayers and gifts which you had offered this year before the divine child, because the help which you give for the Church in need is invariably intended for the same Christ who was once persecuted by Herod in the innocent children. Today he still suffers from the brutalities inflicted on the multitudes which no man can number, from every nation, tribe and race, whose affliction will only end when they have washed their robes white in the blood of the lamb.

Fr. Werenfried van Straaten

Dear friends, what does all this mean for us? What we have said about the nature of God being different, and about the way our lives must be shaped accordingly, sounds very fine, but remains rather vague and unfocused. That is why God has given us examples. The magi from the east are just the first in a long procession of men and women who have constantly tried to gaze upon God's star in their lives, going in search of the God who has drawn close to us and shows us the way. It is the great multitude of the saints – both known and unknown – in whose lives the Lord has opened up the Gospel before us and turned over the pages... They are the shining path which God himself has traced throughout history and is still tracing today.

Pope Benedict XVI
Homily at the vigil with the young people,
World Youth Day, Cologne, 24ᵗʰ August 2005

Two thousand years have now passed. Salvation is no longer proclaimed by the angels of Bethlehem but by sociologists and diplomats. And it is brought about by criminals and men of violence who, once they have smashed everything, call the silence that follows the destruction 'peace' and their unrestrained abuse of power 'freedom'. More than ever we are delivered to Herod.

Fr. Werenfried van Straaten

The magi will no longer ask: How can this serve me? Instead, they will have to ask: How can I serve God's presence in the world? They must learn to lose their life and in this way to find it. Having left Jerusalem behind, they must not deviate from the path marked out by the true king, as they follow Jesus.

Pope Benedict XVI
Homily at the vigil with the young people,
World Youth Day, Cologne, 24th August 2005

Just as once the shepherds brought the Christ child cheese or milk or a warm sheepskin, and just as there were kind-hearted people here and there on the way to Egypt who took pity on the holy family, so it is now our task to help the persecuted Christ of today everywhere he is suffering need in the least of his brothers. For this is the scope of our work: to help all who share the fate of the persecuted Christ child.

Fr. Werenfried van Straaten

Since the first Christmas night the divine child has stretched out his hands to all men. For all men are created in the image of God and are called to become holy, as our father in heaven is holy.

Fr. Werenfried van Straaten

Should there be no room in the inn of our hearts for Christ, after Christmas the injustice will be just as great as ever before.

Fr. Werenfried van Straaten

May Almighty God, who will again brighten the coming Christmas night with the light of his incarnate son, one day let you know the joy of this light in heaven, because you have so earnestly endeavoured to live as new men according to the example of Jesus whose wondrous birth gained victory over our former selves.

Fr. Werenfried van Straaten

The new year that God grants us is an empty space that we must fill in ourselves. What matters most is not what it will bring us but what we make of it. It is like the frame of a picture, on which we must work for a whole year. A picture best painted in bright, cheerful colours – but in which the dark shades are also necessary, because there can be no picture without shadows.

Fr. Werenfried van Straaten

The Christmas trees have gone. The silver ornaments and golden lights, the tinsel and the glass baubles have all been cleared away. What nature gave us we return, dry and faded, to her – young fir trees, after a week of glory now prematurely dead. Let us strive to salvage more than this from the holy season now behind us... Let us now prove ourselves truly 'men of goodwill'. Ahead of us lies a long, long year in which tolerance and sympathy must be our constant companions.

Fr. Werenfried van Straaten

May Almighty God, who will again brighten the coming Christmas night with the light of his incarnate son, one day let you know the joy of this light in heaven, because you have so earnestly endeavoured to live as new men according to the example of Jesus whose wondrous birth gained victory over our former selves.

Fr. Werenfried van Straaten

Yet now [the magi] were bowing down before the child of poor people, and they soon came to realise that Herod, the king they had consulted, intended to use his power to lay a trap for him, forcing the family to flee into exile. The new king, to whom they now paid homage, was quite unlike what they were expecting. In this way they had to learn that God is not as we usually imagine him to be.

Pope Benedict XVI
Priestly ordination in St Peter's, 15th May 2005

Mary, Mother of God

But when the fullness of time had come,
God sent his Son,
born of a woman,
born under the law.
(Galatians 4.4 NAB)

Holy Mary, Mother of God, you have given the world its true light, Jesus, your Son – the Son of God. You abandoned yourself completely to God's call and thus became a wellspring of the goodness which flows forth from him. Show us Jesus, lead us to him. Teach us to know and love him, so that we too can become capable of true love and be fountains of living water in the midst of a thirsting world.

Pope Benedict XVI
Deus Caritas Est, 42

All those whom Christ has redeemed by his blood are children of Mary. Not just the prayerful and the holy, but also the weak and the fainthearted. And the sinners too, and the apostates. Even those who persecute the Faith. As a loving mother, Mary wishes to save us all.

Fr. Werenfried van Straaten

The greatest bulwark that today's destroyers of the Church come up against in their campaign through Christian countries is the doctrines on Mary. These doctrines are more firmly and deeply embedded than many other dogmas in the hearts of the humble, to whom God reveals mysteries which he keeps hidden from the wise and the clever (cf. Mt 11.25).

Fr. Werenfried van Straaten

Now there are priests who blaspheme Mary. They have no love for her. To them can be applied the word of Saint Alphonse that a priest who does not love Mary is a monster. Only monsters can lend themselves to darken in our sexualised world the splendour of the Immaculate Virgin, to abase the God-given image of the mother of God and destroy the last ideal that can preserve weak men from behaving without scruple like animals.

Fr. Werenfried van Straaten

God... He has a mother and is thus truly woven into the tapestry of our human history, so that in fact a woman is able to say to say to him who is her child, a human child: The Lord of the world is within you.

Joseph Cardinal Ratzinger
God and the World, p. 293

We have an immortal soul to save for eternity. Mary calls us to penance and to the prayer of the rosary. It would be foolhardy not to answer her request.

Fr. Werenfried van Straaten

Those who fight on the side of God need fear nothing and no-one. What David accomplished with five stones and a sling, we can now attain according to the word of the Mother of God, with a Rosary, penance and repentance.

Fr. Werenfried van Straaten

As for me, I wish to publicly declare, to the honour of God and of His Holy Mother, that I owe it to the prayer of the Rosary that I did not finally flounder in the storms that assailed and shook my own priestly life, but managed to keep the Faith.

Fr. Werenfried van Straaten

The crumbling of Christian doctrine, the devaluation of the concept of holiness, the rejection of the Evangelical Counsels, the decay of morals, the unfaithfulness of so many priests – and so many other signs of crisis – are worst in those countries where the rejection of Mary, who has overcome all heresies, is at its most radical.

Fr. Werenfried van Straaten

Christians will also give praise to God by rejoicing over people in whom he has shown great and how good he is.

Joseph Cardinal Ratzinger
God and the World, p. 295

Grant, dear Mother, that when we have passed through death's dark gate and stand before the judgment seat of your son, we may find you there with a smile in your eyes, and be able to say without fear: "Hail, Mother".

Fr. Werenfried van Straaten

Mary is with you when you are a sign of contradiction because, by lives of poverty, simplicity, chastity and total dedication to God, you loudly proclaim the Gospel that is passed over in silence. She is with you when you listen to the Pope, whose voice has become like that of one crying in the wilderness. She is with you when you have no other defence left but to pray, to be silent and to forgive. She is with you when you take up your cross and follow Christ.

Fr. Werenfried van Straaten

Mary will not forsake us. The more the lips of those called to preach the truth fall silent, the more numerous are the messages she gives to her chosen ones of pure heart. She gathers the ranks of her humble warriors against the arrogant legion of the proud, who would cast down God from his throne. And whilst the howls of God's enemies increase day by day, she commands her children to respond only with trust, sacrifice, prayer, penance and silence.

Fr. Werenfried van Straaten

Not for the first time, the rejection of Mary has been justified by claiming that to honour her detracts from our love of Christ. The present crisis in the Church refutes the illusion of those who think they can exalt Christ by abasing his mother. It is false to imagine that by discarding Mary our hearts are opened to the influence of Christ.

Fr. Werenfried van Straaten

The darker the night that sinks down over the world, the more brightly shines the light of Mary, showing the seeker and the straying the right way.

Fr. Werenfried van Straaten

On the first day of the year the Church celebrates the great feast of Mary, the Mother of God. In the post-communion prayer we acknowledge that the mother of Christ is also the mother of the Church. That means that Mary will do for the mystical body of Christ, whose members we are, everything that she once did for her son. And just as Jesus entrusted himself entirely to his mother to find safety and protection with her, it is only natural that we too should entrust ourselves to Mary.

Fr. Werenfried van Straaten

Through Mary, and the other holy women, the feminine element stands at the heart of the Christian religion. And this is not in competition with Christ. To think of Christ and Mary as being in competition means ignoring the essential distinction between these two figures. Christ gives John, and through John all of us, the Mother. That is not competition, but a most profound kind of intimacy. The Mother and Virgin forms an essential part of the Christian picture of man.

Joseph Cardinal Ratzinger
God and the World, p. 302

May is the month of Mary, our mother, however weak, sinful and lost we may be. Her blue mantle is so wide that it will always provide one more soft fold to shelter each of her frightened children... including you and me, Werenfried van Straaten.

Fr. Werenfried van Straaten

The image of Mary is distorted by those who never utter her glorious title 'Mother of God', because for them Christ means little more than Buddha, Mohammed or Marx.

Fr. Werenfried van Straaten

Passion and Cross

[Jesus] humbled himself and became obedient unto
death, even death on a cross.
(Philippians 2.8 RSV)

The Cross is the bedrock of Christianity. Whoever refuses to embrace it is powerless against the foes of God.

Fr. Werenfried van Straaten

That man, who wears the crown of thorns and, with it, takes upon himself the crown of the suffering of mankind, is the truly crowned head of all. And what Pilate says has… a very complex meaning over and beyond what he intends to say. Somehow it is saying: 'Yes, that is man', a pitiful worm. At the same time, it shows us the real man, who in his suffering bears the image of God.

Joseph Cardinal Ratzinger
God and the World, p. 332

The cross is not a curse but a blessing and is inseparable from Christianity. Each of us must relive on earth the life of Christ. Therefore our task not only consists in preaching his gospel and practising his love, but above all in sharing personally his sacrifice on the cross, which he continues to offer until the end of time.

Fr. Werenfried van Straaten

It would be a scandal indeed if the young women of our times did not prize or respond to the Cross or to the splendour of a religious vocation, lived for the glory of God and the salvation of souls.

Fr. Werenfried van Straaten

God's will does not alienate us, it purifies us – even if this can be painful – and so it leads us to ourselves. In this way, we serve not only him, but the salvation of the whole world, of all history.

Pope Benedict XVI
Address to mark the official beginning
of his pontificate, 24th April 2005

Less than ever can I do without you. Without your help I – an often weary and sometimes unwilling Simon of Cyrene – should not be able to take the heavy cross of this work of charity every day anew upon my shoulders. Therefore please do not leave me in the lurch!

Fr. Werenfried van Straaten

It is the tremendous event, God really became man. That he did not just disguise himself as man, did not just play the part for a while in history, but that he truly is man – and that finally, when he stretches out his arms on the Cross, he makes himself into a wide open space into which we can enter.

Joseph Cardinal Ratzinger
God and the World, p. 218

The ways of the Lord are not easy, but we were not created for an easy life, but for great things, for goodness.

Pope Benedict XVI
To the German-speaking pilgrims on the day after the
official start of his pontificate, 25th April 2005

If ever a thing was hopeless, then it was the cause that Christ stood for. It was hopeless on Good Friday, when he died on the cross and was buried under a heavy stone. Everything was finished. His enemies returned to routine business. But it was not finished, it was the real beginning. Many times this has been repeated in history. The Church has often been in a seemingly hopeless situation, its epitaph already written. Such is the certainty of those who believe in almighty God and in him whom he has sent: Jesus Christ, our Lord.

Fr. Werenfried van Straaten

If we believe in the Cross, then we must also believe that the blood of the martyrs is the seed of Christians.

Fr. Werenfried van Straaten

Evil can be overcome only by forgiveness. Certainly, it must be an effective forgiveness; but only the Lord can give us this forgiveness, a forgiveness that drives away evil not only with words but truly destroys it. Only suffering can bring this about and it has truly taken place with the suffering love of Christ, from whom we draw the power to forgive.

Pope Benedict XVI
Priestly ordination in St Peter's,
15th May 2005

God comforts us in all afflictions. That is true for you and also for me. Do not be surprised, therefore, when I tell you that along with God's blessings the afflictions, too, have grown very heavy. Often I feel like Ezekiel "in bitterness in the heat of my spirit, the hand of the Lord being strong upon me". (Ez 3.14) Then, to find comfort, I can seek refuge only in the Lord. For I understand the economy of salvation: the Cross which we carry ourselves enables us to comfort others who are in need.

Fr. Werenfried van Straaten

We see the entire structure of the message of Jesus is full of tension; it is an enormous challenge. Its nature is such that it always has to do with the Cross.

Joseph Cardinal Ratzinger
God and the World, p. 225

In the last analysis pain is the product and expression of Jesus Christ's being stretched out from being in God right down to the hell of "My God, why have you forsaken me?" Anyone who has stretched his existence so wide that he is simultaneously immersed in God and in the depths of the God-forsaken creature is bound to be asunder, as it were; such as one is truly 'crucified'. But this process of being torn apart is identical with love; it is its realisation to the extreme (Jn 13.1) and the concrete expression of the breadth it creates.

Joseph Cardinal Ratzinger
Introduction to Christianity, p. 290

Jesus, forsaken and alone on a cross between heaven and earth, has redeemed us all. Only if we love him and are united with him do we possess the ransom for our sins and the key to the kingdom of heaven. Our unity with him should therefore be more precious to us than all treasures on earth.

Fr. Werenfried van Straaten

That is the mystery of God, who did not come into the world as someone who was going to set up a just social order by force of power. He came down to our level in order to suffer for us and with us.

Joseph Cardinal Ratzinger
God and the World, p. 338

Because God himself became a mere worm, the last letter in the alphabet of creation, the last letter has become his letter and thereby turned history toward the final victory of love: the Cross really is the salvation of the world.

Joseph Cardinal Ratzinger
Introduction to Christianity, p. 337

If it was indeed God's will that even Veronica's gesture should not be forgotten after two thousand years, then should we not likewise make every effort to support our suffering brothers and sisters – by a sign from afar, a glance of sympathy, a word of encouragement, a gesture of loving help?

Fr. Werenfried van Straaten

We see the entire structure of the message of Jesus is full of tension; it is an enormous challenge. Its nature is such that it always has to do with the Cross.

Joseph Cardinal Ratzinger
God and the World, p. 225

So great is God's love for man that by becoming man he follows him even into death, and so reconciles justice and love.

Pope Benedict XVI
Deus Caritas Est, 10

You too have your sorrow, your cross, your weakness. Do not let them embitter you. Do not ask to understand what God wishes to conceal from you still. Do not doubt his love. Say with a smile that what God does to you is well done. And let that be your contribution towards the work we are doing together.

Fr. Werenfried van Straaten

This is the task of every Christian – to share from within the Passion of the human condition, so that it may gain space for the presence of God within it.

Joseph Cardinal Ratzinger
Faith and the Future

In Christ, God has bound himself to men, has let himself be bound by them.

Joseph Cardinal Ratzinger
Introduction to Christianity, p. 341

Now that his Calvary has left its bloody traces across the whole world, none but the most selfish and stony-hearted of people can still refuse Christ the service of a Veronica or a Simon of Cyrene that would make them into better persons.

Fr. Werenfried van Straaten

Jesus can grant forgiveness and the power to forgive because he himself suffered the consequences of sin and dispelled them in the flame of his love. Forgiveness comes from the Cross; he transforms the world with the love that is offered. His heart opened on the Cross is the door through which the grace of forgiveness enters into the world. And this grace alone is able to transform the world and build peace.

Pope Benedict XVI
Priestly ordination in St Peter's,
15th May 2005

When Christ speaks of the cross that we ourselves have to carry, it has nothing to do with a taste for torture or of pedantic moralism. It is the impulse of love, which has its own momentum and does not seek itself but opens the person to the service of truth, justice and the good. Christ shows God to us, and thus the true greatness of man.

Pope Benedict XVI
To the German-speaking pilgrims on the day after the
official start of his pontificate, 25th April 2005

I believe that this abandoned Jesus, Who now continues his Passion in the sufferings of millions in East and West, has once more become poor, humiliated and needy so that we can no longer avoid him.

Fr. Werenfried van Straaten

Christ's mercy is not a grace that comes cheap, nor does it imply the trivialisation of evil. Christ carries the full weight of evil and all its destructive force in his body and in his soul. He burns and transforms evil in suffering, in the fire of his suffering love. The day of judgment and the year of favour converge in the Paschal Mystery, in the dead and risen Christ. This is the vengeance of God: he himself suffers for us, in the person of his Son.

Pope Benedict XVI
Mass Pro Elegendo Pontefice, *18th April 2005*

Great and difficult tasks lie ahead of us. But don't lose courage! Rejoice at the miracles with which God is blessing our work and be thankful that you, with your prayers and donations, are among the countless Veronicas and Simons of Cyrene who, for all your human weakness, are called to accompany and help Jesus to follow the Ways of the Cross of the Church in need.

Fr. Werenfried van Straaten

On Mount Horeb, Elijah was made to understand that God is not in the wind, the earthquake or the fire; Elijah has to learn and perceive the soft voice of God, and in this way to recognise in advance the One who overcame sin not with power but by his Passion; the One who, by his suffering, has given us the ability to forgive. This is how God wins.

Pope Benedict XVI
Priestly ordination in St Peter's,
15th May 2005

To [God] we can and we must bring, in complete honesty, the whole burden of our life. We are rather too inclined to forget that in the book of Job, handed down to us in Holy Scripture, at the end of the drama God declares Job to be righteous – Job, who has hurled the most outrageous accusations at God – while He rejects Job's friends as speakers of falsehood, those friends who had defended God.

Pope Benedict XVI
What it means to be a Christian, p. 20

Anyone who has inwardly accepted suffering becomes more mature and more understanding of others, becomes more human.

Joseph Cardinal Ratzinger
God and the World, p. 322

Although the Cross is foolishness and a stumbling block to the unbelieving generation whose voice is often raised so loud in the Church today, for countless numbers of the faithful – the sick, the lonely, the misunderstood, the aged, those who fear for the Church, the oppressed and the persecuted – it is still the height of wisdom, and they are unwavering in their loyalty to it. It is thanks to them that our heavenly father can still see his beloved son in the spiritual wilderness of today and refrains from cursing his faithless people for ever.

Fr. Werenfried van Straaten

How often we wish that God would show himself stronger, that he would strike decisively, defeating evil and creating a better world. All ideologies of power justify themselves in exactly this way, they justify the destruction of whatever would stand in the way of progress and the liberation of humanity. We suffer on account of God's patience. And yet, we need his patience. God, who became a lamb, tells us that the world is saved by the Crucified One, not by those who crucified him. The world is redeemed by the patience of God. It is destroyed by the impatience of man.

Pope Benedict XVI
Address to mark the official beginning
of his pontificate, 24th April 2005

At his hour in the garden of Gethsemane, Jesus transformed our rebellious human will into a will conformed and united with the divine will. He suffered the whole drama of our independence – and by placing our will in God's hands, he gives us true freedom: "Not as I will, but as you will." (Mt 26.39) Our redemption is brought about in this communion of wills: being friends of Jesus we become friends of God. The more we love Jesus, the more we know him, the more our true freedom develops and our joy in being redeemed flourishes. Thank you, Jesus, for your friendship!

Pope Benedict XVI
Mass Pro Elegendo Pontefice, *18th April 2005*

I believe we only understand the Beatitudes correctly if we understand them from the viewpoint of the person of Christ. It is in him they are lived out, and it is through him that they are able to show us the way. In all this, individual callings are of course various. For one person one of them will stand out, and for someone else, another one. It is important to understand them as being embodied in the figure of Christ and thus to find they can be lived out in following him.

Joseph Cardinal Ratzinger
God and the World, p. 285

In the Way of the Cross, we cannot merely be spectators. We too are involved, so we must seek our place: where are we? In the Way of the Cross, it is impossible to remain neutral. Pilate, the sceptic intellectual, tried to be neutral, to remain uninvolved; but precisely in this way he took a stance against justice, because of the conformism of his career.

Pope Benedict XVI
Good Friday Address in the Colosseum,
14th April 2006

Christ's life is the standard for each Christian life. In spite of weakness and fear we are called to re-live his life and die his death and thereafter share his victory.

Fr. Werenfried van Straaten

We have seen that on the Way of the Cross, Paul found the zeal of his faith and kindled the light of love. We have seen how St Augustine found his way: as well as Francis of Assisi, St Vincent de Paul, St Maximilian Kolbe and Mother Teresa of Calcutta. So it is that we too are invited to find our place, to discover with these great, courageous saints, the way with Jesus and for Jesus: the way of goodness and truth; the courage of love.

Pope Benedict XVI
Good Friday Address in the Colosseum,
14th April 2006

Easter and Resurrection

"Do not be afraid; for I know that
you seek Jesus who was crucified.
He is not here; for he has risen, as he said.
Come, see the place where he lay."
(Matthew 28. 5-6 RSV)

Our Easter faith gives us hope that the risen Lord will truly transform the world. In his resurrection we recognise the fulfilment of God's promise to the exiled people of Israel: "I will open your graves and raise you from your graves, O my people; and I will bring you home into the land of Israel." (Ez 37.12)

Pope Benedict XVI
To the members of the Papal Foundation,
5th May 2006

Those who meet the risen Jesus are inwardly transformed; it is impossible 'to see' the Risen One without 'believing' in him. Let us pray that he will call each one of us by name and thus convert us, opening us to the 'vision' of faith.

Pope Benedict XVI
General audience, 18th April 2006

If the Church tells us that the Eucharist is an essential part of Sunday, this is no mere positivism or thirst for power. On Easter morning, first the women and then the disciples had the grace of seeing the Lord. From that moment on, they knew that the first day of the week, Sunday, would be his day, the day of Christ the Lord. The day when creation began became the day when creation was renewed. Creation and redemption belong together. That is why Sunday is so important.

Pope Benedict XVI
Homily at the vigil with the young people,
World Youth Day, Cologne, 24th August 2005

If the Church, with an unshakeable faith in the resurrected Christ, continues his divine life on earth, it cannot possibly be weaker than 'the world' and will never be destroyed either by eastern atheism or western materialism and neo-modernism. But everywhere where the sheep in imitation of the shepherds no longer believe in the spiritual power of the Church, it is lost.

Fr. Werenfried van Straaten

Is there a gaping chasm between the alleluias and reality? Is the Easter alleluia a meaningless empty cry? No! The Church Militant, to which we all belong, stands in the midst of the reality of warring mankind. The alleluia is hers, through faith in the Cross and Resurrection. It is the victory chant of the Christ who died and – against all the laws of nature – rose again, who reconciles us with God and gives us his own life, so that with him we may defy this terrible epoch.

Fr. Werenfried van Straaten

The Eucharist makes constantly present the risen Christ who continues to give himself to us, calling us to participate in the banquet of his body and his blood. From full communion with him flows every other element of the Church's life: first of all, communion among all the faithful, the commitment to proclaiming and witnessing to the Gospel, the ardour of love for all, especially the poorest and lowliest.

Pope Benedict XVI
First homily as Pope, 20th April 2005

Mission

"I must preach the good news of the
kingdom of God to the other cities also;
for I was sent for this purpose."
(Luke 4.43 RSV)

The Church is by nature missionary; her urgent duty is to evangelise.

Pope Benedict XVI
Visit to the Basilica of St Paul
Outside-the-Walls, 25th April 2005

The Catholic Church... asks no privileges for herself but only the legitimate conditions of freedom to carry out her mission. In the concert of nations, she always seeks to encourage understanding and cooperation between peoples based on loyalty, discretion and friendliness.

Pope Benedict XVI
To the ambassadors of the diplomatic corps
accredited to the Holy See, 12th May 2005

In a certain sense, one does not become a Christian for oneself at all; rather one does so for the sake of the whole, for others, for everyone. The movement of becoming a Christian, which begins at baptism and which we have to pursue through the rest of our lives, means being ready to engage in a particular service that God requires from us in history.

Pope Benedict XVI
What it means to be a Christian, p. 54

The hunger for God in the East and the rejection of God in the West now demand a new evangelisation.

Fr. Werenfried van Straaten

Serving the Gospel should not be considered a solitary adventure but a commitment to be shared by every community. As well as those who are in the front line on the frontiers of evangelisation – and I am thinking here with gratitude of the men and women missionaries – many others, children, young people and adults, with their prayers and cooperation, contribute in various ways to spreading the kingdom of God on earth. It is to be hoped that this participation will continue to grow, thanks to the contribution of one and all.

Pope Benedict XVI
Message for World Mission Sunday,
29th April 2006

Dear Brothers in the Episcopate, in a time such as our own, marked by the growing phenomenon of globalisation, it is ever more necessary to make the truth about Christ and his Gospel of salvation reach everyone. There are countless fields in which to proclaim and witness lovingly to the truth; multitudes are thirsting for it and cannot be allowed to waste away in search of food (cf. Lam 4.4). This is our mission.

Pope Benedict XVI
To the members of the 11th ordinary council of the General Secretariat of the Synod of Bishops,
1st June 2006.

We cannot bring to the world the good news which is Christ himself in person if we ourselves are not deeply united with Christ, if we do not know him profoundly, personally, if we do not live on his words.

Pope Benedict XVI
Address held at the conclusion of the annual Lenten retreat for the Roman Curia, 11ᵗʰ March 2006

May Mary, Star of Evangelisation, help and sustain those in many regions of the world who work on the front lines of the mission. In this regard, how could one forget those who, also recently, have given their life for the Gospel? May their sacrifice obtain a renewed springtime, rich in apostolic fruit for evangelisation.

Pope Benedict XVI
Address to mark the 40th anniversary of the conciliar decree 'Ad Gentes', 11ᵗʰ March 2006

This is the great alternative that we must learn over and over again: to give priority to our own expectations, rejecting Jesus, or to accept Jesus in the truth of his mission and set aside all too human expectations.

Pope Benedict XVI
General audience, 17ᵗʰ May 2006

Anyone who has discovered Christ must lead others to him. A great joy cannot be kept to oneself. It has to be passed on.

Pope Benedict XVI
Address to mark the 40th anniversary of the conciliar decree
'Ad Gentes', 11th March 2006

Being missionaries means loving God with all one's heart, even to the point, if necessary, of dying for him. How many priests, men and women religious and lay people, have borne the supreme witness of love with martyrdom even in our times! Being missionaries means stooping down to the needs of all, like the good Samaritan, especially those of the poorest and most destitute people, because those who love with Christ's heart do not seek their own interests but the glory of the Father and the good of their neighbour alone. Here lies the secret of the apostolic fruitfulness of missionary action that crosses frontiers and cultures, reaches peoples and spreads to the extreme boundaries of the world.

Pope Benedict XVI
Message for World Mission Sunday,
29th April 2006

Prayer

O Lord, let your ear be attentive to
the prayer of this your servant
and to the prayer of your servants
who delight in revering your name.
(Nehemiah 1.11 NIV)

Whenever someone opens himself for God in prayer, then he enters into his special closeness.

Joseph Cardinal Ratzinger
God and the World, p. 107

The Lord is always within hearing. We can inwardly draw away from him. We can live turning our backs on him. But he always waits for us and is always close to us.

Pope Benedict XVI
Mass and Installation in the Chair of the Bishop of Rome. Lateran Basilica, 7th May 2005

Satan is engaged in an all-out war. On all fronts, and especially in the secrecy of our hearts, he is fighting to extinguish the light of God. Therefore he must be driven out from every corner of our lives – and at once! So do not put off banishing the Devil with prayer and fasting.

Fr. Werenfried van Straaten

Worship means accepting that nothing finite can be my goal or determine the direction of my life, but that I myself must pass beyond all possible goals. That is, pass beyond them into being inwardly at one with him who wished me to exist as a partner in a relationship with him and who has given me freedom precisely in this.

Joseph Cardinal Ratzinger
God and the World, p. 111

Pray for me, that I may not flee for fear of the wolves. Let us pray for one another, that the Lord will carry us and that we will learn to carry one another.

Pope Benedict XVI
Mass for the inauguration of the pontificate,
24th April 2005

Together with Mary, the mother of Jesus, the apostles persevered as one in prayer. The answer was the miracle of Pentecost, in Jerusalem, where 3,000 people were baptised in a day. So too when we persevere in prayer, inspired by faith, hope and love – together with Mary, the Pope and the true apostles (who also exist in our own day) and with the greatest possible number of priests, religious, fathers, mothers and other Christians of good will – then miracles will occur again today.

Fr. Werenfried van Straaten

Let us go and pray to the Lord to help us bear fruit that endures. Only in this way will the earth be changed from a valley of tears to a garden of God.

Pope Benedict XVI
Mass Pro Elegendo Pontefice, *18th April 2005*

Pray with unshakeable trust and with a heart that embraces both friend and foe in love. And the Lord will stoop down to us and his mercy will know no bounds.

Fr. Werenfried van Straaten

We... find in the Holy Scriptures this business of God hiding. God hides from disobedient people. He is silent. He does not send any prophets. And in the lives of saints, too, there is this dark night. They are, so to speak, thrust into a kind of absence, the silence of God, as for instance happened to Thérèse of Lisieux, and they then have to share in the darkness of the unbeliever.

Joseph Cardinal Ratzinger
God and the World, p. 107

Every bastion and stronghold of persecution and distortion of the Faith must be besieged by legions of humble souls, willing to concentrate their prayers on these tyrants and false prophets who seek to destroy the kingdom of God.

Fr. Werenfried van Straaten

Before any activity, before the world can change, there must be worship. Worship alone sets us truly free; worship alone gives us the criteria for our action. Precisely in a world in which guiding criteria are absent and the threat exists that each person will be a law unto himself, it is fundamentally necessary to stress worship.

Pope Benedict XVI
Christmas greetings to the members of
the Roman Curia, 22nd December 2005

The Evangelists tell us that the Lord frequently withdrew – for entire nights – "to the mountains", to pray alone. We too need these "mountains": they are inner peaks that we must scale, the mountain of prayer.

Pope Benedict XVI
Chrism Mass, Holy Thursday in
St Peter's, Rome, 13th April 2006

We are not powerless against the dangers that threaten the world today. For we can storm Heaven with our prayers, begging God to shorten the time of trial. We can deny ourselves something or bear with love whatever burden Our Lord imposes upon us. We can adopt a soul in need and carry their sorrows in our prayer. We can rise again from our sins so that others, at the end of their strength, can find the courage not to succumb to evil. And by giving up not only what we have to spare, but even occasionally the necessities, we can provide the material help to save them from despair.

Fr. Werenfried van Straaten

People who pray are not wasting their time, even though the situation appears desperate and seems to call for action alone. Piety does not undermine the struggle against the poverty of our neighbours, however extreme.

Pope Benedict XVI
Deus Caritas Est, 36

It is necessary to enter into real friendship with Jesus in a personal relationship with him and not to know who Jesus is only from others or from books, but to live an ever deeper personal relationship with Jesus, where we can begin to understand what he is asking of us. And then, the awareness of what I am, of my possibilities: on the one hand, courage, and on the other, humility, trust and openness, with the help also of friends, of Church authority and also of priests, of families: what does the Lord want of me?

Pope Benedict XVI
Meeting with the young people of
the diocese of Rome, 6th April 2006

Holy martyrs, I ask your intercession for the Church in need. I am counting on the prayers of the spiritually rich, on the intercession of Mary and on the blessing of Almighty God. Don't delay in helping us; time is pressing…

Fr. Werenfried van Straaten

Spending time in God's presence in prayer is a real pastoral priority; it is not an addition to pastoral work: being before the Lord is a pastoral priority and in the final analysis, the most important. John Paul II showed this to us in the most practical and enlightened way in every circumstance of his life and ministry.

Pope Benedict XVI
Meeting with the priests and deacons of the diocese of Rome
in the Lateran Basilica, 13th May 2005

Let our contribution for the Church in need be an act of penance, a real renunciation, a sacrifice that hurts. And let us pray the rosary more faithfully than ever in the month of October, in which for ages past menaced Christianity has sought refuge in Mary.

Fr. Werenfried van Straaten

May the Divine Mercy, the measure of which we ourselves determine through the kindness we show to our neighbour, be ours even now in an abundance of grace. Then, fortified by this grace, we will be able to avoid sin, overcome our weakness, bring God's plans to fulfilment in us and grow out of ourselves and into the full stature of the loving Christ, who is good and patient, who sows goodness in his path and who, even from the Cross, promises us Paradise.

Fr. Werenfried van Straaten

There is no need to be discouraged on account of the fact that prayer requires effort, or because of the impression that Jesus remains silent. He is indeed silent, but he is at work. In a world where there is so much noise, so much bewilderment, there is a need for silent adoration of Jesus concealed in the Host. Be assiduous in the prayer of adoration and teach it to the faithful. It is a source of comfort and light particularly to those who are suffering.

Pope Benedict XVI
Meeting with the clergy in the Cathedral
of St John, Warsaw, Poland, 25th May 2006

The Lord is always within hearing. We can inwardly draw away from him. We can live turning our backs on him. But he always waits for us and is always close to us.

Pope Benedict XVI
Mass and Installation in the Chair of the Bishop of Rome.
Lateran Basilica, 7th May 2005

God has never let us down! But only a rock-like trust will guarantee that our prayers are heard; a trust that must be proved by living deeds. That is why our prayer for peace and reconciliation will only be heard if we first prepare ourselves for it with deeds of peace and reconciliation.

Fr. Werenfried van Straaten

Let us beseech the Lord to reawaken in us the joy at his presence and that we may once more adore him. Without adoration, there is no transformation of the world.

Joseph Cardinal Ratzinger
God Is Near Us, p. 93

One should not read Scripture in an academic way, but with prayer, saying to the Lord: "Help me to understand your word, what it is that you want to tell me in this passage".

Pope Benedict XVI
Meeting with the young people of
the diocese of Rome, 6th April 2006

Faith

Now faith is the assurance of things hoped for,
the conviction of things not seen.
(Hebrews 11.1 RSV)

The basic pattern of Christian faith is not: 'I believe something', but: 'I believe in you.'

Joseph Cardinal Ratzinger
Faith and the Future

Christ demands a faith that will move mountains. And since he never demands the impossible we can, in the strength of our faith, move aside mountains of misery and ignorance, of misunderstanding, hatred and selfishness. Usually this implies a task of reconciliation, which can be achieved only through prayer, humility and selfless love.

Fr. Werenfried van Straaten

Since Abraham and until the return of the Lord, faith advances to meet him who is coming. But in Christ the countenance of him who is to come is already revealed: it will be the man who can embrace all men because he has lost himself and them to God.

Joseph Cardinal Ratzinger
Introduction to Christianity, pp. 242-243

Faith is always a venture that cannot be reconciled with earthly securities. The man who has secured himself on all sides no longer has any need to look to others, to depend on them or be grateful to them. He is self-sufficient. But his cold world of self-sufficiency stands in contradiction to the world of love.

Fr. Werenfried van Straaten

God demands our total abandonment, something that to human wisdom might seem reckless, but to the wisdom of God means complete security in him, who is all-good and all-powerful.

Fr. Werenfried van Straaten

We must choose our path afresh each day. The imitation of the humble, submissive and obedient Christ in His Hidden Life is a sure way…

Fr. Werenfried van Straaten

I am only a true believer if faith is present within me as a living seed, from which something is growing and which then truly changes my world and, in doing so, brings something new into the world as whole.

Joseph Cardinal Ratzinger
God and the World, p. 46

The word Gospel means Good News. In its most concise form it means that we must love God Our Father above all things and our neighbour as ourselves. This was the message that Christ proclaimed by His Life and Death. "Woe to me if I do not proclaim the Gospel!" says St. Paul. And woe to us likewise, if we are not good news for one another or pleasing in the sight of God, by virtue of our kindness and mercy in word and deed. Woe to us if we do not proclaim the Gospel!

Fr. Werenfried van Straaten

After having experienced God's blessing, helping us or saving us in the most difficult situations and over so many years, I cannot ultimately distinguish where trust in God ends and recklessness begins.

Fr. Werenfried van Straaten

He who admits, for all his own failures, that God's demands are just, is honest. Dishonest is the man – and that is characteristic of our times – who tailors truth to his own way of living, who raises his own lifestyle to a standard, who denies the validity of moral laws because he himself does not keep them.

Fr. Werenfried van Straaten

It is impossible to proclaim his Gospel in such a way that no one is offended, except by suppressing certain truths. This is impermissible and can be of no advantage to us in our work. For a person who writes or preaches in terms so veiled as not to offend will likewise be unable to console or to inspire.

Fr. Werenfried van Straaten

The countries of the so-called Christian west have in the past – and not only in the past – done great harm by their bad example. We too belong to the 'civilised nations' which show the still 'uncivilized peoples' a spectacle that often drives them away from Christianity.

Fr. Werenfried van Straaten

Living from faith is more like striding up a mountainside than sitting dreaming by the fireside. But whoever opts for the journey that this involves knows, and experiences more and more, that the adventure to which it invites us is indeed worthwhile.

Joseph Cardinal Ratzinger
Faith and the Future

Only when Christ becomes the sole norm of our actions, only when we do what he did and reject what he rejected, only when his love of God and of mankind shines forth constantly in our actions, only when the heavenly father can recognize his Christ in us and when countless searching or misguided souls can discover their redeemer in our actions – only then will his kingdom be truly re-established on earth.

Fr. Werenfried van Straaten

In his First Letter, St Peter, the first Bishop of Rome, says that we Christians must be ready to explain our faith. This presupposes that we ourselves have understood the reason of faith, that we have truly 'digested', even rationally, with the heart, with the wisdom of heart, this word that can truly be an answer for others.

Pope Benedict XVI
Meeting with the priests and deacons of the diocese of Rome
in the Lateran Basilica, 13th May 2005

Holy Church is not a collection of cultural monuments, but the living Christ, who wishes to be in *our* hearts and give with *our* hands and be good in *our* love.

Fr. Werenfried van Straaten

Years of experience have taught us that all the wonderful things that Christ has taught us about the goodness and faithfulness of our Heavenly Father are quite literally true.

Fr. Werenfried van Straaten

For the believer, it is impossible to imagine that God is powerless or that "perhaps he is asleep"…

Pope Benedict XVI
Deus Caritas Est, 38

It is heartening to know that God never accepts the loss of those who are to be his for all eternity. Although no one has ever seen him and he dwells in inaccessible light, he does not hesitate to leave his lonely place and take upon himself the painstaking search for his lost sheep. He is the unfathomable being who leaves his heavenly splendour to run calling after his straying lambs. He caused Gospels to be written, full of parables proclaiming his concern for all poor and lost creatures. This concern also include the lost sheep of our time.

Fr. Werenfried van Straaten

There will be moments in life when, in all kinds of darkness, our Faith is truly condensed into a simple yes: I believe in you, Jesus of Nazareth; I am confident that in you is manifested that divine perspective from which I can confidently and calmly, patiently and courageously face up to my life.

Joseph Cardinal Ratzinger
Faith and the Future

Let yourselves be swept along by God's grace. For he calls on us now, through the Pope and through so many prophets, to reform our lives and renew our love. And he tells us too that our western world, racked by apostasy, rebellion, rationalism and immorality, can only be regained for Christ if many of us return to the steep and narrow path of authentic Christianity.

Fr. Werenfried van Straaten

Remaining steadfast in the teaching of the apostles... receiving the word from the living Church, keeping it alive, and passing it on. You can do that only if you live together in her, if your life is directed to her true heart, finding in her the earth in which to root your life, and being able then, ever and again, to hand it on to men.

Joseph Cardinal Ratzinger
God Is Near Us, p. 125

It is my conviction, as I have often stated, that the true apologetics of the Christian faith, the convincing proof of its truth – despite all the negative aspects – are on the one hand the saints and on the other the beauty that the Faith has produced. If faith is to grow today, then we must bring ourselves and the people we meet into the encounter with the saints, into contact with this beauty.

Pope Benedict XVI
From a message to
'Communion & Liberation', 2002

It was not by chance that I myself, an ailing student who had been declared unfit for military service and for the Capuchins, was given the fighting name of Werenfried – "warrior for peace" – although by nature I was anything but suited to fight for peace in the work that God was later to entrust to me. God demands the impossible. Like the harsh king in the gospel he demands back what he has not given and would reap what he has not sown. So he required David to beat Goliath. So he overtaxed his apostles to the extent that after his ascension they shut themselves up in the upper room in fear and trembling. So he harasses the whole Church, that fragile ship, in the storm which he still is not ready to calm. So he wanted my name to be Werenfried.

Fr. Werenfried van Straaten

The path of least resistance has already led to disaster, for all too many people. So let us listen instead to the voice of Jesus: "Enter by the narrow gate, for the gate is wide and the way is easy that leads to destruction, and those who enter by it are many. But the gate is narrow and the way is hard that leads to life, and those who find it are few." (Mt 7.13-14)

Fr. Werenfried van Straaten

Allow me to reassure you that, in the mystery of salvation, the mystery of evil always serves a useful end.

Fr. Werenfried van Straaten

The existence with Christ inaugurated by faith is the start of resurrected life and therefore outlasts death (cf. Phil 1.23; 2 Cor 5.8; 1 Thess 5.10). The dialogue of faith is itself already life, which can no longer be shattered by death.

Joseph Cardinal Ratzinger
Introduction to Christianity, pp. 334-335

Only those who in blind trust try to do every moment the will of God can face the future fearlessly.

Fr. Werenfried van Straaten

Where God is no longer present, holes appear which no one and nothing can fill – holes in legislation, in men's hearts, in morals and in social life.

Fr. Werenfried van Straaten

The more Satan succeeds in weakening our organisation, the more it will correspond to the yardstick Saint Paul has given to us, for "God chose what is foolish in the world to shame the wise, God chose what is weak in the world to shame the strong…"

Fr. Werenfried van Straaten

Only faith, repentance and conversion to God can save us. For God alone can rescue us from evil. That is why all efforts to achieve peace and unity in the world will be futile unless we – both you and I – earnestly desire to become better Christians.

Fr. Werenfried van Straaten

We have performed a masterpiece of diplomacy in reconciling Christ with the world, in falsifying his way of life – which should be the standard for every Christian – and in adapting his unavoidable demands to our human weakness. His light does indeed shine in the darkness, but where is the John who will bear witness to this light with living deeds?

Fr. Werenfried van Straaten

What is most alarming about our situation, and the most serious weakness within the Church, is the decay of the Christian spirit among us all – we who should make Christianity attractive and desirable to future generations, instead of compromising it as we so often do. We must return to Christ.

Fr. Werenfried van Straaten

Faith is not just a ready-made guarantee, something one can regard as accumulated capital that can only grow. Faith is always given only in the context of a fragile freedom. We may wish it were otherwise. But just therein lies God's great gamble, which we find so hard to understand, that he has not given us stronger medicine.

Joseph Cardinal Ratzinger
God and the World, p. 55

This preaching of the faith we can promote by our spiritual and material aid to those who are preparing the way for the Lord, who wishes to clothe with his power and his glory even the modern slaves in Latin America so that there may be neither slave nor freeman but all will be one in him. For where the God-Man becomes visible in his members, miracles happen.

Fr. Werenfried van Straaten

What faith actually means for man is not something that can be portrayed in the abstract. It can only be rendered visible in those people who have lived this outlook consistently to the end – in Francis of Assisi, in Francis Xavier, Ignatius of Loyola, Teresa of Avila... Faith too, as can be seen in such figures, is essentially a particular kind of passion or, rather, a love that consumes a person and shows him a path that he must follow, even when this path is difficult.

Joseph Cardinal Ratzinger
Faith and the Future

Faith means resisting the brute force that would otherwise pull us under. Faith means fellowship with him who has the other kind of power, one that draws us, that holds us fast, that carries us safely over the elements of death.

Joseph Cardinal Ratzinger
God and the World, p. 241

Does not our Lord demand a faith that can move mountains? If he is not a madman asking for the impossible this means that in the power of our faith we can also move mountains of misery and have no right to shirk this task.

Fr. Werenfried van Straaten

The one thing I most want to share with you, from my full and busy life, is this: the Gospel is true. Never has Our Lord abandoned me. He has always helped me and granted what I asked him for the Church in need. On this is based my boundless trust. It has become my second or, better still, my true nature.

Fr. Werenfried van Straaten

Only God can save us; God alone. But God will only save us if we are worth saving, if we become again his people, his children... We ourselves know what we must change in our lives, what we must confess. Let us wait no longer. It is high time. Let us at last become better people and convince God that we are worth the trouble of saving.

Fr. Werenfried van Straaten

I should be neglecting my priestly duty if I only wrote begging letters and ignored the spiritual dangers threatening our Christianity.

Fr. Werenfried van Straaten

Faith in God is not a form of knowledge that can be learned like chemistry or mathematics, but remains a belief. That is, it has a perfectly rational structure... It is not just some dark mystery or other with which I have dealings. It gives me insight. And there are perfectly comprehensible reasons for accepting it. But it is never simply knowledge.

Joseph Cardinal Ratzinger
God and the World, p. 33

At its very core, faith is not a system of knowledge but a matter of trust. Christian faith is "the discovery of a You" who can carry me and, in all the unfulfilment and ultimate unfulfillability of the human encounter, grant me the promise of an indestructible love that not only desires, but actually grants eternity.

Joseph Cardinal Ratzinger
Faith and the Future

Instead of being a rock of unanimity and loyalty in the tempest of darkness, we weaken the Church through our conformity with the world, through disobedience and opposition to the Pope, through new heresies, new schisms and embittered fraternal strife.

Fr. Werenfried van Straaten

The life of the Church can never be other than the eternally new unfolding of Jesus' life on earth.

Fr. Werenfried van Straaten

Today, when there is more talk than prayer, when every priest has to be turned into a social reformer and every layman into a dialogue-hungry theologian, the Church of Silence fulfils an essential task.

Fr. Werenfried van Straaten

I think that one has never achieved complete faith. Faith has to be lived again and again in life and in suffering, as well as in the great joys that God sends us. It is never something that I can put in my pocket like a coin.

Joseph Cardinal Ratzinger
God and the World, p. 23

An 'adult' faith is not a faith that follows the trends of fashion and the latest novelty; a mature adult faith is deeply rooted in friendship with Christ. It is this friendship that opens us up to all that is good and gives us a touchstone by which to distinguish the true from the false, and deceit from truth. We must develop this adult faith; we must guide the flock of Christ to this faith.

Pope Benedict XVI
Mass Pro Elegendo Pontefice, 18th April 2005

Sadly, many people have become all too wise, and so clever in their reasoning that both the Gospel and such childlike faith in God's providence have been rationalised right out of existence. Their cleverness has an answer for everything – except the miracles that Jesus has promised to those of faith and fearless trust in God. They would rather re-interpret the Gospel than admit that all is not well with their own personal faith.

Fr. Werenfried van Straaten

Is it not foolish to beseech a grace of God without being prepared to cooperate with this grace?

Fr. Werenfried van Straaten

Our Christianity must once more become ardent and glowing – the city on the hill top and the light on the lamp stand – so that others will recognise where truth and life are to be found!

Fr. Werenfried van Straaten

We must not remain children in faith, in the condition of infant. And what does it mean to be children in faith? St Paul answers: it means being "tossed here and there, carried about by every wind of doctrine." (Eph 4.14) This description is very timely!

Pope Benedict XVI
Mass Pro Elegendo Pontefice, *18th April 2005*

I am convinced that God also permits all this suffering for our sakes, so that at the Last Judgement Jesus can say to us: "What you have done for the least of my brothers, you have done for Me." (cf. Mt 25.40) And none of us, bombarded with information as we are by all the media, can then turn to him and say: "Lord, when did we see you hungry or thirsty, or persecuted, beaten up or homeless, naked, sick or imprisoned, betrayed and abandoned by all – even by the great powers – and did not help you?" (cf. Mt 25.44)

Fr. Werenfried van Straaten

If we are to gaze on God's Glory forever with him and attain perfect happiness, then we must first of all 'adapt' to him. For even we humans cannot live side-by-side forever unless we are well suited to one another. And so we must be imbued with the same outlook, the same wisdom and the same spirit as that which imbued Christ himself.

Fr. Werenfried van Straaten

Will Christ really come? Yes, he will come with his grace, so as to live more fully in us. He will come, if we are ready to welcome him and cooperate with his grace. Then, but only then, will we be the doors through which he enters the world. Only then can we lend him the form in which he will become visible.

Fr. Werenfried van Straaten

We too must trust in the Lord, the mighty, strong God, who mocks the heathen and shatters him like vessels of clay. It is not dangerous to build on him alone, for he has overcome the world. Let us soothe him by our guileless trust and by the waves of our prayer, beating confidently on the shores of eternity and breaking like surf on his attentive heart.

Fr. Werenfried van Straaten

Faith can lose its way if I only pray according to mood and whim. Faith also needs discipline of the dry periods; then something grows in the silence. Just as in the winter fields, despite appearances, the growth lies hidden.

Joseph Cardinal Ratzinger
God and the World, p. 320

Being a Christian means allowing Christ to be made manifest in us and bearing his shining image through these times, even through the tempest that now assails God's kingdom on earth and may even destroy it here and there. This is a task that exceeds our strength. God himself must intervene.

Fr. Werenfried van Straaten

What catastrophes will break over us unless we succeed in giving today's youth, torn loose from its moorings, a future and an ideal? This is a test case for Christianity, because Christ dies and rose for this youth too.

Fr. Werenfried van Straaten

Today there are millions of people whom dire need has distanced from God, and millions who reject God because they feel abandoned by him. But even Jesus himself needed an angel to comfort him when he feared death, and so God will be merciful to all the disillusioned who did not feel the touch of this angel's wings. For them the mystery of suffering is so dark, they cannot glimpse the glow of God's love concealed in it. A kind word, an understanding glance, a little sympathy, a spark of love may well be enough to bring them nearer to God again.

Fr. Werenfried van Straaten

The image of Moses, who had to climb up the mountain and go into the cloud to find God, remains valid for all ages. God cannot be found – even in the Church – except by our climbing the mountain and entering into the cloud of the incognito of God, who in this world is the hidden One.

Pope Benedict XVI
What it means to be a Christian, p. 37

Nowadays there are priests and professors who, blinded by doubts or unbelief, no longer see what the Lord expects of his bride, the Church, and therefore try to discover in sociology or in dialogue with atheists what the world expects of her. They forget that for a Church which is not subordinate to God not a single task remains in the world which cannot be done just as well or better by pagans.

Fr. Werenfried van Straaten

Naturally, I am aware and we all know that many are not immediately able to identify themselves with, to understand, to assimilate all that the Church teaches. It seems to me important firstly to awaken this intention to believe with the Church... It is necessary to have this will to believe with the Church, to have trust that this Church... truly carries within herself the 'compass' of the Spirit and therefore is the true subject of faith. The individual, then, is inserted into this subject, adheres to it, and so, even if he or she is still not completely penetrated by this, the person has trust and participates in the faith of the Church, wants to believe with the Church.

Pope Benedict XVI
Meeting with the priests and deacons of the diocese of Rome in the Lateran Basilica, 13th May 2005

I cannot make Christ my private possession and try to keep him for myself. To a certain extent, the discomfort of belonging to his family goes along with Christ himself. Faith has been bestowed on us in this community context; it is not otherwise available.

Joseph Cardinal Ratzinger
God and the World, p. 68

God too is better than we think! All the wonderful things that Jesus taught us about the goodness of our heavenly father are literally true. God has never shamed my trust!

Fr. Werenfried van Straaten

We do not persecute Christ, but we compromise him. As long as we detract from Christ's splendour with our materialism and selfishness, we shall not have the strength to draw the disillusioned communists and all the searching people of our times to him who so fervently desires to reign in their hearts too.

Fr. Werenfried van Straaten

Hope

The Lord is good to those whose hope is in him,
to the one who seeks him.
(Lamentations 3.25 NIV)

Faith, hope and love are ultimately all one, and all those things around which faith revolves are only concrete expressions of the overwhelming transformation, of the "I believe in You" – of the discovery of God in the features of the man, Jesus of Nazareth.

Joseph Cardinal Ratzinger
Faith and the Future

God is present, then, wherever faith and hope and love are, because they, contrary to what happens with sin, constitute the personal space within which we move into the dimensions of God. Thus God is present in a quite specific sense in every place where something good is happening, a sense that goes beyond his general omnipresence and his comprehension of all being. He may be encountered as a more profound presence wherever we approach those dimensions of existence that most closely correspond to this inner being – namely, those of truth and love, of goodness of any kind.

Joseph Cardinal Ratzinger
God and the World, p. 107

God searches the heart and loins. He knows the extent of our confidence. He knows if we are really ready to place our trust in the message of Jesus... Therefore he often strips us of all earthly hope in order to be himself, our only hope. He demands our unconditional abandonment.

Fr. Werenfried van Straaten

The person in a difficult situation will hold on if he knows 'God is there first and loves me'. And that is the trustworthy ground on which my life is standing and on which I myself can construct it.

Joseph Cardinal Ratzinger
God and the World, p. 26

God has never disappointed our trust in him. Again and again he has helped us to fulfil the promises – often rash ones from a human point of view – that we have made to the Church in need for his sake.

Fr. Werenfried van Straaten

It is not a stranger who judges us but he whom we know in faith. The judge will not advance to meet us as the entirely Other, but as one of us, who knows human existence from inside and has suffered. Thus over the judgment glows the dawn of hope…

Joseph Cardinal Ratzinger
Introduction to Christianity, p. 327

The theological virtue of hope is indispensable for every pilgrim on the way to his heavenly home. This hope – the absolutely certain expectation of eternal blessedness – does not rest on human promises but on the promises of the infinitely faithful and almighty God.

Fr. Werenfried van Straaten

I fear that, in our striving on behalf of God's Kingdom, we all too often forget the theological virtues of faith, hope and charity. Once every child would learn these acts of virtue by heart. Who knows or prays them now? And yet without this bond with God, the Church – which is a theocracy – becomes degraded into a sort of democratic association, a secularised ecclesiastical state, soon turned by political quarrelling and manipulated opinion polls into a divided kingdom.

Fr. Werenfried van Straaten

Love

He who does not love does not know God;
for God is love.
(1 John 4.8 RSV)

Whoever loves is another Christ.

Pope Benedict XVI
What it means to be a Christian, p. 69

God imbues the entire creation and human history with his love.

Pope Benedict XVI
Message for World Mission Sunday,
29th April 2006

Need cries out again and again for help, and you are always ready to respond, because God, who is boundless Love, chose to entrust you with his work of love. To me he has granted the boldness to beg without limits, and to you the readiness to give without limits. Let us humbly acknowledge the privilege of being allowed to participate in Jesus' redemptive work like this, for it is not due to our own merit, but to the Grace of God.

Fr. Werenfried van Straaten

What we renounce out of love belongs to God in any case. And if we ourselves belong to him, we may yet perhaps overcome the power of darkness. For love is stronger than death.

Fr. Werenfried van Straaten

Love towards our enemies demands that we pray for them without ceasing, in the sure hope that they will be converted.

Fr. Werenfried van Straaten

Love is the greatest of all commandments. Sometimes indeed, through original sin, through our wounded nature, through predisposition, circumstance, inherited faults, or lured by the siren voices of false theologians, we are too open to the deceitful promptings of the devil. But just along as we can still say, like fallen Peter, that we truly love our Lord, and as long as we continue to help him when he pleads, hungry or poor, naked, sick or beaten by thieves, for our support and comfort in the least of his brethren – then we will yet be able to stand with confidence before his judgment seat, trusting in his promise: "Blessed are the merciful, for they shall obtain mercy."

Fr. Werenfried van Straaten

Being a Christian means having love. That is unbelievably difficult and yet, at the same time, incredibly simple.

Pope Benedict XVI
What it means to be a Christian, p. 72

Love should be measureless, boundless. It should be ready not only to provide the bare necessities for our brothers in need but also, after the example of our heavenly father, to give "the rest that shall be added unto you".

Fr. Werenfried van Straaten

The more we love Jesus, the more we know him, the more our true freedom develops and our joy in being redeemed flourishes. Thank you, Jesus, for your friendship!

Pope Benedict XVI
Mass Pro Elegendo Pontefice, *18th April 2005*

True love is expressed in acts that exclude no one, after the example of the Good Samaritan who, with great openness of heart, helped a stranger in difficulty whom he had met "by chance" along the way (cf. Lk 10.31).

Pope Benedict XVI
Homily on Ash Wednesday, 1st March 2006

Aid to the Church in Need was born in a storm of generosity. Its motive power was love, kindled in multitudes of hearts and spreading like a wildfire. This love was stronger than hatred and worked miracles of forgiveness.

Fr. Werenfried van Straaten

Truth and love coincide in Christ. To the extent that we draw close to Christ, in our own lives too, truth and love are blended. Love without truth would be blind; truth without love would be like "a clanging cymbal".

Pope Benedict XVI
Mass Pro Elegendo Pontefice, *18th April 2005*

The love that comes from God, that he himself sets flowing from heart to heart as a manifestation of his goodness, shares in God's immensity and never thinks it has done enough.

Fr. Werenfried van Straaten

At the Last Judgment we will hear the verdict: "Come ye blessed of my father, inherit the kingdom prepared for you" or "Depart from me, ye accursed, into the eternal fire" (Mt 25.31-46), depending on whether we have treated our neighbour, with whom the son of God identifies himself, with love or without love. For let us not deceive ourselves: Christianity cannot possibly go hand in hand with hatred, enmity or lack of love.

Fr. Werenfried van Straaten

In Christ the beauty of truth and the beauty of love converge; but love, as people know, also calls for the willingness to suffer, a willingness which for those who love one another can even extend to the sacrifice of life! (cf. Jn 15.13) Christ, who is "the beauty of every beauty", as St Bonaventure used to say (*Sermones Dominicales*, 1.7), is made present in the hearts of men and women and attracts them to their vocation which is love.

Pope Benedict XVI
Address to World Congress of Ecclesial Movements and New Communities, 22nd May 2006

We must be enlivened by a holy restlessness: a restlessness to bring to everyone the gift of faith, of friendship with Christ. Truly, the love and friendship of God was given to us so that it might also be shared with others. We have received the faith to give it to others – we are priests in order to serve others. And we must bear fruit that will endure.

Pope Benedict XVI
Mass Pro Elegendo Pontefice, *18th April 2005*

The extraordinary fusion between love of God and love of neighbour makes life beautiful and causes the desert in which we often find ourselves living to blossom anew.

Pope Benedict XVI
Address to World Congress of Ecclesial Movements and New Communities, 22nd May 2006

There is a tragic passage in the Holy Scripture: "He came to his own, and his own received him not." There was no place for him because "his own" were without love. This is the dark root of all wars and destruction, all wrongs and disorders.

Fr. Werenfried van Straaten

Being a Christian means having love; it means achieving the Copernican revolution in our existence, by which we cease to make ourselves the centre of the universe, with everyone else revolving around us.

Pope Benedict XVI
What it means to be a Christian, p. 73

Love... demands that we try to love as God loves. He loves us, not because we are especially good, particularly virtuous or of any great merit, not because we are useful or even necessary to him; he loves us, not because *we* are good, but because *he* is good. He loves us, although we have nothing to offer him; he loves us even in the ragged raiment of the prodigal son, who is no longer wearing anything lovable.

Pope Benedict XVI,
What it means to be a Christian, p. 69

If we deny love, we deny God and these words of scripture will apply to us: "By your fault God's name is blasphemed among the gentiles..."

Fr. Werenfried van Straaten

Without Christ, everything goes wrong, because he is the head governing the whole of mankind. And Christ is present only where there is love.

Fr. Werenfried van Straaten

Please do not think only of yourselves, like Pilate or the conscienceless high priests in Jerusalem, but comfort the man of sorrows with your love. God will then be pleased with you and his peace will be with you.

Fr. Werenfried van Straaten

Those who die in love will be crowned by God's love.

Fr. Werenfried van Straaten

Our believing and our loving are still on their way, so long as we remain in this world, and again and again they are in danger of flickering out... No one can say of himself: "I am completely saved." In the era of this world there is no redemption as a past action, already completed; nor does it exist as a complete and final present reality; redemption exists only in the mode of hope.

Pope Benedict XVI
What it means to be a Christian, p. 84

Being a Christian means essentially changing over from being for oneself to being for one another.

Joseph Cardinal Ratzinger
Introduction to Christianity, p. 252

Love is possible, and we are able to practise it because we are created in the image of God.

Pope Benedict XVI
Deus Caritas Est, 39

Where the fire of love is extinguished, the night of hatred breaks in, turning men into wolves whose inhumanity daily fills us with consternation on every TV screen... Yet we must not look only at the hatred and murder. We must also see the love which, despite all the atrocities, still exists; the love which consoles the dying, binds up wounds and comforts the afflicted. The love in all the Gulags, the refugee camps and the slums of this world.

Fr. Werenfried van Straaten

Without love all prayer, all self-mortification, all piety is no more than self-deception or hypocrisy – which God detests.

Fr. Werenfried van Straaten

It is God, who governs the world, not we. We offer him our service only to the extent that we can, and for as long as he grants us the strength. To do all we can with what strength we have, however, is the task which keeps the good servant of Jesus Christ always at work: "The love of Christ urges us on." (2 Cor 5.14)

Pope Benedict XVI
Deus Caritas Est, 35

Love itself is a passion, something we endure. In love I experience first a happiness, a general feeling of happiness. Yet, on the other hand, I am taken out of my comfortable tranquility and have to let myself be reshaped.

Joseph Cardinal Ratzinger
God and the World, p. 322

Do not be afraid! Our salvation is in our own hands. For the Prince of Darkness is not to be feared because he opposes God, but because we forget God; not because he is strong in hate, but because we are weak in love; not because he kills Christians, but because we do not live as Christians and are shackled to this earth with a thousand chains.

Fr. Werenfried van Straaten

By abiding in the love of Christ we learn, at the school of Christ, the art of true love.

Pope Benedict XVI
Funeral Mass for his Holiness John Paul II,
8th April 2005

Please help us to play our part in the Pope's final attempt to make the Christian family a place of shelter for love, which can then be carried out into the world. Then at last there will be parents willing once more to bear with joy the burden of a large family and welcoming it as an honour, not fearing it as a nightmare, when God chooses one of their children for his service.

Fr. Werenfried van Straaten

When we know that the way of love... is the true way by which man becomes human, then we also understand that suffering is the process through which we mature.

Joseph Cardinal Ratzinger
God and the World, p. 322

Christianity is great because love is great. It burns, yet this is not a destructive fire but one that makes things bright and pure and free and grand.

Joseph Cardinal Ratzinger
God and the World, p. 221

God did not create evil, for he is Love, and on the evening of each day of creation he found that everything was good. He certainly did not will evil; nor did he prevent it – not wishing to destroy the supreme benefit of human freedom – and also because even sin is serviceable in his almighty hand. He is more ingenious than we are. Every time we shatter what he has made, the pieces fall together again in a still finer mosaic, in which his wisdom shines yet brighter than before.

Fr. Werenfried van Straaten

Pain is a part of being human. Anyone who really wanted to get rid of suffering would have to get rid of love before anything else, because there can be no love without suffering, because it always demands an element of self-sacrifice, because, given temperamental differences and the drama of situations, it will always bring with it renunciation and pain.

Joseph Cardinal Ratzinger
God and the World, p. 322

Love is never 'finished' and complete; throughout life, it changes and matures, and thus remains faithful to itself.

Pope Benedict XVI
Deus Caritas Est, 17

Yet I remain an optimist, because God never fails in his providence and always attains his end with unerring certainty. He who is Love never ceases, through the outpouring of the Holy Spirit, to fill the whole earth with the love of Jesus, through all those who continue his life.

Fr. Werenfried van Straaten

Anyone who wishes to give love must also receive love as a gift. Certainly, as the Lord tells us, one can become a source from which rivers of living water flow (cf. Jn 7.37-38). Yet to become such a source, one must constantly drink anew from the original source, which is Jesus Christ, from whose pierced heart flows the love of God (cf. Jn 19.34).

Pope Benedict XVI
Deus Caritas Est, 7

Only our love can persuade the nations, to whom the future belongs, to accept the inheritance that God has entrusted to us. This inheritance is not western culture or modern technology, but the Gospel, the Church and the Sacraments. The preservation of these immeasurable riches of faith and grace for the future is the greatest and most vital task before us.

Fr. Werenfried van Straaten

We all have something to make up for, because we all have fallen short in love and concern for our poor brothers, of whom we so seldom think.

Fr. Werenfried van Straaten

Never may the love of neighbour displace the love of God, which is our response to the Almighty and to his appearance in Christ. For however inhuman it is to forget our neighbour and profess to love only God, it is much worse to declare that God is dead and abolish love of him, while loving man alone and treating man as God. This is not love of neighbour, in fact, but idolatry.

Fr. Werenfried van Straaten

I am only fulfilling my mission to love, so to speak, when I become the person I am capable of being; when I am giving what I am able to give; when I open up those possibilities in creation and in the network of human relationships that help us to get through life together and together to shape the fertile capacity of the world and of life into a garden, in which we can find both security and freedom.

Joseph Cardinal Ratzinger
God and the World, p. 190

We may indeed claim that our charity benefits not only the persecuted refugee Christians from the east but, far more, the nations of the west. Countless people have discovered and learned the essence of Christianity in Aid to the Church in Need, as in a school of love.

Fr. Werenfried van Straaten

You don't have to learn loving in the same way as you learn, for instance, to play the piano or how to use a computer. You have to learn it as you go, so to speak, in this sphere or that. And of course you also learn from people who offer you role models. First of all from your parents, who offer you both example and guidance and in whom you see what it is to be human. Later you learn through friendship; you learn through some task that brings you into contact with someone, through some mission. In all this it is not a matter of seeking for oneself but of learning the way of giving and, thereby, the right way to receive.

Joseph Cardinal Ratzinger
God and the World, p. 191

True pity... is a kind of identification with the suffering of another, and thus it is a true and essential act of love.

Joseph Cardinal Ratzinger
God and the World, p. 196

The love-story between God and man consists in the very fact that this communion of will increases in a communion of thought and sentiment, and thus our will and God's will increasingly coincide: God's will is no longer for me an alien will, something imposed on me from without by the commandments, but it is now my own will, based on the realisation that God is in fact more deeply present to me than I am to my self.

Pope Benedict XVI
Deus Caritas Est, 17

The Gospel has been printed in every language. But the hungry people need more than a paper Gospel. They need a living Gospel, just as Christ was the living Good News. They hunger for living souls in whom Christ is made manifest, in whom they can recognise and love Christ himself.

Fr. Werenfried van Straaten

If I have no contact whatsoever with God in my life, then I cannot see in the other anything more than the other, and I am incapable of seeing in him the image of God.

Pope Benedict XVI
Deus Caritas Est, 18

We must not live according to the wisdom of the world – which to God is foolishness (1 Cor 3.19) – but according to the wisdom and spirit of God, which is a spirit of love.

Fr. Werenfried van Straaten

Acknowledgement of the living God is one path towards love, and the 'yes' of our will to his will unites our intellect, will and sentiments in the all-embracing act of love.

Pope Benedict XVI
Deus Caritas Est, 17

Without love, the most radical sharing out of earthly riches is worthless.

Fr. Werenfried van Straaten

This love covers over many a sin. Only when God sees this love in us will he take us up to his heavenly home, even though our lives were full of weaknesses and sins.

Fr. Werenfried van Straaten

It is not pain as such that counts but the breadth of the love that spans existence so completely that it unites the distant and the near, bringing God-forsaken man into relation with God. It alone gives the pain an aim and a meaning.

Joseph Cardinal Ratzinger
Introduction to Christianity, p. 291

Only if you have love can Christ meet you too and say: "Peace be with you!" Where there is no love peace is impossible. There is no other way out but love.

Fr. Werenfried van Straaten

Love of God and love of neighbour are thus inseparable, they form a single commandment. But both live from the love of God who has loved us first... Love grows through love. Love is 'divine' because it comes from God and unites us to God; through this unifying process it makes us a 'we' which transcends our divisions and makes us one, until in the end God is "all in all." (1 Cor 15.28)

Pope Benedict XVI
Deus Caritas Est, 18

It cannot possibly be that our love for the suffering Christ can have no influence in the kingdom of God. The Church is a system of interconnecting vessels. No one lives for himself alone.

Fr. Werenfried van Straaten

Christ has said that he has come to bring fire on earth. It was not only Palestine and Sudan he had in mind but also the modern world in which we live. He is constantly returning with the flame of his love, which he places in our hearts to make them like his own. Only thus can we make the new year that God has given us light and warm for our brothers who live in cold and darkness.

Fr. Werenfried van Straaten

In acknowledging the centrality of love, Christian faith has retained the core of Israel's faith, while at the same time giving it new depth and breadth. The pious Jew prayed daily the words of the Book of Deuteronomy which expressed the heart of his existence: "Hear, O Israel: the Lord our God is one Lord, and you shall love the Lord your God with all your heart, and with all your soul and with all your might." (Deut 6.4-5) Jesus united into a single precept this commandment of love for neighbour found in the Book of Leviticus: "You shall love your neighbour as yourself." (Lev 19.18; cf. Mk 12.29 ff.)

Pope Benedict XVI
Deus Caritas Est, 1

Have we still the inward strength to continue Christ's work of redemption and to apply it to this youth? Are we still Christians? Have we still that love, that selfless love of our neighbour which is the only true mark of the Christian? Without this love our Christianity is a lie, by which we draw down on ourselves the curse of God. But with this love we are able to renew the face of the earth.

Fr. Werenfried van Straaten

Those who wish to make peace with Nazis, capitalist exploiters, communists or other sinners must practise love to the utmost. They may not, however, excuse evil or barter the rights of the downtrodden for a false peace. For there can be no peace without justice.

Fr. Werenfried van Straaten

Love of neighbour can exist only in and through the love of God. It is based on the words: "What ye have done to the least of my brethren ye have done unto me." It derives its victorious power from the fact that God's son, who is infinitely lovable, has identified himself with the least of his brethren. They share in his lovableness. They have a right to the love we owe to him. Those who consider this love superfluous take away the reason for loving them. They degrade love, in all its sublime holiness, to a humanitarian gesture of which even heathens are capable.

Fr. Werenfried van Straaten

Christ told his story about the rich glutton, not because of that one beggar who, long before in Abraham's bosom, had been alleviated of his afflictions, but because of the Lazaruses of today who starve in their millions at the very doors of our affluence.

Fr. Werenfried van Straaten

The Judge does not ask what kind of theory a person has held about God and the world. He is not asking about a confession of dogma, solely about love. That is enough, and it saves a man. Whoever loves is a Christian.

Pope Benedict XVI
What it means to be a Christian, pp. 68-69

Charity

And now there remain these
faith, hope and charity:
But the greatest of these is charity.
(1 Corinthians 13.13 Douai-Rheims)

Wherever one person does something good for another, there God is especially near.

Joseph Cardinal Ratzinger
God and the World, p. 107

The pastoral character of our work is the distinctive feature that gives Aid to the Church in Need a special place among the many charitable initiatives that developed in the Church after the war... We have never relinquished this pastoral character of our work – not even when it became fashionable to put social progress above the narrow path to Heaven, development aid above missionary work, violent liberation above redemption via the Cross, the material above the spiritual and the temporal above the eternal.

Fr. Werenfried van Straaten

For the Church, charity is not a kind of welfare activity which could equally well be left to others, but is a part of her nature, an indispensable expression of her very being.

Pope Benedict XVI
Deus Caritas Est, 25a

It is a great joy to me to ascertain that the vast majority of you do not only trust me as a beggar but also as a priest. It is my fervent desire in these times of confusion to do something for your spiritual welfare.

Fr. Werenfried van Straaten

Without doubt we [ACN] are acting contrary to human wisdom when each January, despite our empty coffers and bank accounts, we promise hundreds of bishops to finance the thousands of projects they have entrusted to us with tens of millions of dollars over the coming three, six or twelve months. But to me, as a penniless religious in 1947, the only possible way of bringing immediate help to the poor outcasts entrusted to my care was precisely this – by making promises which in themselves were an immediate source of hope and encouragement and which – as I firmly trusted – were fulfilled by the grace of God with lightning speed by countless faithful souls.

Fr. Werenfried van Straaten

The more people we can open fire upon – I mean the fire of love – the greater will be the number of burning hearts for the Church in distress.

Fr. Werenfried van Straaten

Like Paul, who wanted to be a Greek with the Greeks and a Jew with the Jews, I must adapt myself to my flock. I cannot therefore fob off the hundreds of thousands who in their spiritual loneliness expect a priestly word from me with the slogans now currently in vogue. He who writes in these unsettled times so diplomatically that he hurts no one's sensitivities will not be able either to comfort or to inspire anyone.

Fr. Werenfried van Straaten

It is not easy to rejoice in suffering for Christ's sake. It is true that the cross loses its weight when we surrender to the will of God, and that our love of Christ gives us strength to bear crosses that seem unbearable. Undoubtedly God still chooses the weak to confound the strong. But as with the first Christians, who comforted one another, today too God has provided human help for our suffering brothers. This task of helping has been entrusted to our work.

Fr. Werenfried van Straaten

Turn within yourself and look God in the eyes. Would you dare to look your own father in the face if you had allowed your brothers and sisters to perish without raising a hand to help them?

Fr. Werenfried van Straaten

The love that emanates from God, that is made manifest in Christ and that is granted to us as a gift of God, is more than a humanitarian gesture. Without it the best of mankind remains as "sounding brass and tinkling cymbals". Without it the most progressive social reforms and the most radical redistribution of earthly wealth is worthless. For "although I bestow all my goods to feed the poor (and this is a great humanitarian work)... and have not charity, it profiteth me nothing."

Fr. Werenfried van Straaten

"Whatsoever you did to one of the least of my brothers, you did to me". These words should be dearer to us than all earthly wisdom. Despite all our shortcomings, they should spur us on to seek unremittingly for opportunities to love the Lord in the poor, in whose form he is concealed.

Fr. Werenfried van Straaten

Our responsibility is great. Just one kind word, a slice of bread or perhaps the holy fire in the eyes of a priest may determine whether the name of Christ will be blessed or cursed. We can betray the image of Christ within us. We can be a path to Christ, or we can be a barrier blocking this path.

Fr. Werenfried van Straaten

Saint Paul, in his hymn to charity (cf. 1 Cor 13) teaches us that it is always more than activity alone: "If I give away all I have, and if I deliver my body to be burned, but do not have love, I gain nothing." (v.3) This hymn must be the *Magna Carta* of all ecclesial service... Practical activity will always be insufficient, unless it visibly expresses a love for man, a love nourished by an encounter with Christ. My deep personal sharing in the needs and sufferings of others becomes a sharing of my very self with them: if my gift is not to prove a source of humiliation, I must give to others not only something that is my own, but my very self; I must be personally present in my gift.

Pope Benedict XVI
Deus Caritas Est, 34

Fear is a poor counsellor. Many have an unreasonable fear of the future. They are always concerned about imminent catastrophes, which they look upon as a consequence of the sins of others, and take precautions to escape them. But perhaps they themselves are lacking in kindness, mercy or peacefulness. Perhaps they sin against charity. Perhaps they lose their inner peace and their spiritual view of things, so that they no longer see what God wants of them.

Fr. Werenfried van Straaten

We must love each other and help each other, like St. Martin. He was riding his horse; a beggar cried for help; but St. Martin had nothing left to give. So he took his cloak, cut it in half and gave one half to the beggar. Half, reader! The beggar was Christ. Every poor man is Christ.

Fr. Werenfried van Straaten

What matters with regard to our aid campaigns is not what we *can* do, but what we *must* do. For we can do *all* things by the power of the One who gives us strength.

Fr. Werenfried van Straaten

You cannot personally journey along the roads where we carry out the Samaritan's task. We do it in your name and with your money.

Fr. Werenfried van Straaten

Deny yourself a cigarette, a glass of wine, a visit to the cinema; deny yourself something that is in fact a superfluous luxury. The money you save is no longer yours... Give it to the persecuted Church, through the intermediary of Aid to the Church in Need. We assure you we can turn it into effective relief!

Fr. Werenfried van Straaten

Charity, like love that renews all things, moves from God's heart to the heart of Jesus Christ, and through his Spirit across the world. This love is born from the encounter with Christ in faith: "Being Christian is not the result of an ethical choice or a lofty idea, but the encounter with an event, a person, which gives life a new horizon and a decisive direction." (Deus Caritas Est, 1)

Pope Benedict XVI
To the participants of the Plenary Assembly of
the Congregation for the Doctrine of the Faith,
10th February 2006

Love – *caritas* – will always prove necessary, even in the most just society. There is no ordering of the State so just that it can eliminate the need for a service of love. Whoever wants to eliminate love is preparing to eliminate man as such. There will always be suffering which cries out for consolation and help. There will always be loneliness.

Pope Benedict XVI
Deus Caritas Est, 28b

I have made our charity into a school of love, in which we have together learned to help the poor and to become better ourselves – better men, who prove their love of God by their care for their fellow men, in whom God's image is hidden.

Fr. Werenfried van Straaten

Persevere in prayer and in charity – fruits which you should attribute not to me but to God, who merely uses my words as a vehicle of his grace. For the goodness which inspires your giving finds its origin in the heart of God.

Fr. Werenfried van Straaten

Many of the poor who come knocking at the doors of parish communities to ask for the help they need to get through moments of serious difficulty often come from countries very far from Italy. Welcome these brothers and sisters with great warmth and willingness, and do all you can to help them in their need, always remembering the Lord's words: "As you did it to one of the least of these my brethren, you did it to me." (Mt 25. 40)

Pope Benedict XVI
To the permanent deacons of the diocese of Rome,
18th February 2006

Charity does not mean fine-sounding phrases; it means deeds and sacrifices. It claims a part of our very selves.

Fr. Werenfried van Straaten

Nowadays very little is said, even in sermons and Church newsletters, about this supernatural dimension of Christian brotherly love. The reason is that fewer and fewer Christians allow themselves to be guided by supernatural motives. In many cases one can no longer speak of Christian charity, but at best of humanitarian generosity. Many people have forgotten that every act of Christian love must be a glorification of God and must ultimately be directed towards Christ, who wishes to be loved in the least of his little ones.

Fr. Werenfried van Straaten

We are not ashamed to harass you because we know that, through our intermediary, Christ himself is spurring you to generous love for the least of his brethren. In his name we stretch out our hands to you for help. There is no danger of your giving too much because God can demand everything of you all and of Werenfried van Straaten.

Fr. Werenfried van Straaten

In today's spiritual confusion, to which there is still no end in sight, we must offer the Christian faithful clarity, security, consolation and courage. Only then will those who seek God help us, with amazing generosity, to continue the work entrusted to us by the Church.

Fr. Werenfried van Straaten

People are far better than we think. They await only the burning word that will enkindle their hearts. They are prepared to show heroic courage if only we have the courage to ask genuine sacrifices of them and convince them that these sacrifices are truly necessary for the kingdom of God.

Fr. Werenfried van Straaten

Whereas most other charities have come into being in response to hunger, disease, poverty, illiteracy and natural disasters, our concern is directed above all at the spiritual and religious need into which countless people are plunged. Our help is ultimately directed towards the salvation of immortal souls. That is why we are a pastoral organisation.

Fr. Werenfried van Straaten

The Church can never be exempted from practising charity as an organised activity of believers...

Pope Benedict XVI
Deus Caritas Est, 28

Charity... cannot be used as a means of engaging in what is nowadays considered proselytism. Love is free; it is not practised as a way of achieving other ends. But this does not mean that charitable activity must somehow leave God and Christ aside. For it is always concerned with the whole man.

Pope Benedict XVI
Deus Caritas Est, 31c

I have disturbed the comfortable consciences of the good citizens in God's kingdom, who see the Church as a welfare state in which they can safely live for the salvation of their souls, without a care for others.

Fr. Werenfried van Straaten

We who belong to the prosperous Church and are proud of being adult, know that the time for anathemas is gone and that we are obliged, even without constraints, to transform the social teaching of the Church into actions. But woe to us if we fail to do so. For we are a minority. The majority are the poor and the uneducated.

Fr. Werenfried van Straaten

I love all 600,000 of you. For God has given you to me as a gift and as sharers in the task that we labour at together… Without you the flame of hope would long have been extinguished in many hearts. Without you I would never have found the strength to continue this work in the troubles that have chastened us.

Fr. Werenfried van Straaten

Let us ensure that our charity remains a refuge of love. For only if we do so can consolation, hope, encouragement and a spirit of reconciliation go out from it into the whole world, for the glory of God and the joy of millions of suffering souls, including that of your grateful friend, Werenfried van Straaten.

Fr. Werenfried van Straaten

We see that every pound and every dollar of all the millions you entrust to us goes out with the stamp of love on it. Only this love shelters us from all the wolves and tyrants threatening God's defenceless flock and opens for us the way to eternal life.

Fr. Werenfried van Straaten

In the name of God and on behalf of countless of our brothers and sisters, who have experienced the consolation of your love, I thank you! For the light which burns through the faith in your souls is reflected in your good works.

Fr. Werenfried van Straaten

Holy Eucharist

For my flesh is true food,
and my blood is true drink.
(John 6.55 NAB)

The Eucharist is peace from the Lord.

Joseph Cardinal Ratzinger
God Is Near Us, p. 117

In Holy Communion we receive Christ in the form of bread. In the poor that we meet we receive him in the form of flesh and blood. It is the same Christ.

Fr. Werenfried van Straaten

The Church is eucharistic fellowship. She is not just a people: out of the many peoples of which she consists there is arising one people, through the one table that the Lord has spread for us all. The Church is, so to speak, a network of eucharistic fellowships, and she is united, ever and again, through the one Body we all receive.

Joseph Cardinal Ratzinger
God Is Near Us, p. 115

"Feed my sheep," says Christ to Peter... Feeding means loving, and loving also means being ready to suffer. Loving means giving the sheep what is truly good, the nourishment of God's truth, of God's word, the nourishment of his presence, which he gives us in the Blessed Sacrament.

Pope Benedict XVI
Mass for the inauguration of the pontificate,
24th April 2005

The Eucharist is far more than just a meal; it has cost a death to provide it, and the majesty of death is present in it. Whenever we hold it, we should be filled with reverence in the face of this mystery, with awe in the face of this mysterious death that becomes a present reality in our midst. Certainly, the overcoming of this faith in the Resurrection is present at the same time, and we can therefore celebrate this death as the feast of life, as the transformation of the world.

Joseph Cardinal Ratzinger
God Is Near Us, p. 44

In the Eucharist, we ourselves learn Christ's love. It was thanks to this centre and heart, thanks to the Eucharist, that the saints lived, bringing to the world God's love in ever new ways and forms. Thanks to the Eucharist, the Church is reborn ever anew!

Pope Benedict XVI
Mass and Installation in the Chair of the Bishop of Rome, Lateran Basilica, 7th May 2005

For the celebration of the Eucharist is not just a meeting of heaven and earth; rather, it is also a meeting of the Church then and now and a meeting of the Church here and there; it assumes that we visibly enter into a visible unity, one that can be described. The name of the bishop and the pope stand for the fact that we are truly celebrating the one Eucharist of Jesus Christ, which we can receive only in the one Church.

Joseph Cardinal Ratzinger
God Is Near Us, p. 53

The highest form of pastoral action is the Holy Sacrifice of the Mass.

Fr. Werenfried van Straaten

Wherever the Eucharist is celebrated, [Jesus] is wholly and fully present. Because of that, even in the most humble village church, when the Eucharist is celebrated, the whole mystery of the Church, her living heart, the Lord, is present. But this Christ, fully present, is yet at the same time one. That is why we can receive him together with everyone else. He is the same, here or in Rome, in America or in Australia or in Africa.

Joseph Cardinal Ratzinger
God Is Near Us, p. 52

Here [in the Eucharist] is the central act of transformation that alone can truly renew the world: violence is transformed into love, and death into life. Since this act transmutes death into love, death as such is already conquered from within, the Resurrection is already present in it. Death is, so to speak, mortally wounded, so that it can no longer have the last word. To use an image well known to us today, this is like inducing nuclear fission in the very heart of being – the victory of love over hatred, the victory of love over death.

Pope Benedict XVI
Homily at the concluding Mass of the 20th World Youth Day, Cologne, Germany, 21st August 2005

What happens to bread and wine in the Eucharist is more profound; it is more than a change of use. The Eucharist transcends the realm of functionality. That is in fact the poverty of our age, that we now think and live only in terms of function, that man himself is classified according to his function, and that we can all be no more than functions and officials, where being is denied. The significance of the Eucharist as a sacrament of faith consists precisely in that it takes us out of functionality and reaches the basis of reality. The world of the Eucharist is no game; it does not rest on conventions, to which we agree and which we can also renounce; but here it is a matter of reality, of its fundamental basis.

Joseph Cardinal Ratzinger
God Is Near Us, p. 88

Eternal life, which takes its beginning in communion with God here and now, seizes this here and now and takes up within the great expanse of true reality, which is no longer fragmented by the stream of time. There, the mutual impermeability of I and thou can no longer exist, as this is closely associated with the fragmentation of time. In fact, anyone who sets his will within the will of God deposits it right there, where all good will has its place; and thus our will blends with the will of all others. Wherever this happens, the saying becomes true: I live, and yet no longer I – Christ lives in me.

Joseph Cardinal Ratzinger
God Is Near Us, p. 143

We all eat the one bread, and this means that we ourselves become one. In this way, adoration… becomes union. God no longer simply stands before us as the One who is totally Other. He is within us, and we are in him. His dynamic enters into us and then seeks to spread outwards to others until it fills the world, so that his love can truly become the dominant measure of the world.

Pope Benedict XVI
Homily at the concluding Mass of the 20th World Youth Day, Cologne, Germany, 21st August 2005

The body and blood of Christ are given to us so that we ourselves will be transformed in our turn. We are to become the body of Christ, his own flesh and blood. We all eat the one bread, and this means that we ourselves become one.

Pope Benedict XVI
Homily at the concluding Mass of the 20th World Youth Day, Cologne, Germany, 21st August 2005

Presiding in doctrine and presiding in love must in the end be one and the same: the whole of the Church's teaching leads ultimately to love. And the Eucharist, as the love of Jesus Christ present, is the criterion for all teaching.

Pope Benedict XVI
Mass and Installation in the Chair of the Bishop of Rome, Lateran Basilica, 7th May 2005

If we think and live according to our communion with Christ, then our eyes will be opened. Then we will no longer be content to scrape a living just for ourselves, but we will see where and how we are needed.

Pope Benedict XVI
Homily at the concluding Mass of the 20th World
Youth Day, Cologne, Germany, 21st August 2005

The Church is none other than that network – the Eucharistic community! – within which all of us, receiving the same Lord, become one body and embrace all the world.

Pope Benedict XVI
Mass and Installation in the Chair of the Bishop
of Rome, Lateran Basilica, 7th May 2005

Jesus and the Sacraments

This is how you should think of us:
as servants of Christ and the stewards
of the Sacraments of God.
(1 Corinthians 4.1)

Christ takes nothing, and he gives everything.

Pope Benedict XVI
Address to mark the official beginning
of his pontificate, 24th April 2005

Let us [priests] reflect once again on the signs in which the Sacrament [of Ordination] has been given to us. At the centre is the very ancient rite of the imposition of hands, with which he took possession of me, saying to me: "You belong to me." However, in saying this he also said: "You are under the protection of my hands. You are under the protection of my heart. You are kept safely in the palm of my hands, and this is precisely how you find yourself in the immensity of my love. Stay in my hands, and give me yours."

Pope Benedict XVI
Chrism Mass, Holy Thursday
in St Peter's, Rome, 13th April 2006

Let us fix our gaze ever anew on him and reach out to him. Let us allow his hand to take ours, and then we will not sink but will serve the life that is stronger than death and the love that is stronger than hatred. Faith in Jesus, son of the living God, is the means through which, time and again, we can take hold of Jesus' hand and in which he takes our hands and guides us.

Pope Benedict XVI
Chrism Mass, Holy Thursday
in St Peter's, Rome, 13th April 2006

The Sacrament of Penance is one of the Church's precious treasures, since the authentic renewal of the world is accomplished only through forgiveness. Nothing can improve the world if evil is not overcome.

Pope Benedict XVI
Priestly ordination in St Peter's,
15th May 2005

What we believe is important, but even more important is the One in whom we believe.

Pope Benedict XVI
Homily at the Mass in Blonie Park,
Krakow, Poland, 27th May 2006

The Lord removes the dirt from us with the purifying power of his goodness. Washing one another's feet means above all tirelessly forgiving one another, beginning together ever anew, however pointless it may seem. It means purifying one another by bearing with one another and by being tolerant of others; purifying one another, giving one another the sanctifying power of the Word of God and introducing one another into the Sacrament of Divine Love.

Pope Benedict XVI
Mass of the Lord's Supper,
Holy Thursday, 13th April 2006

The Lord gives us his hand, lifts us up and heals us. And he does so in all ages; he takes us by the hand with his Word, thereby dispelling the fog of ideologies and forms of idolatry. He takes us by the hand in the sacraments, he heals us from the fever of our passions and sins through absolution in the Sacrament of Reconciliation. He gives us the possibility to raise ourselves, to stand before God and before men and women.

Pope Benedict XVI
Pastoral visit to the parish of St Anne
at the Vatican, 5th February 2006

The Sacrament of Marriage is not an invention of the Church; it is really 'consecrated' with man as such, as a fruit of the dynamism of love in which the man and the woman find themselves and thus also find the Creator who called them to love.

Pope Benedict XVI
Meeting with the young people of
the diocese of Rome, 6th April 2006

Kingdom

"The kingdom of the world has become the kingdom
of our Lord and of his Christ, and he shall reign for
ever and ever."
(Apocalypse 11.15 RSV)

The first necessity is Christ. He is the kingdom of God and the inalienable domain in which God is completely the master. Only those who share his life by faith and grace are citizens of this kingdom and have a part both in the pleasure God takes in him and in the power that is given to Christ also on earth.

Fr. Werenfried van Straaten

Everything in heaven and on earth would be empty were it not for God, who has made himself our portion forever. "This is eternal life, that they know you the only true God, and Jesus Christ whom you have sent," says the Lord in the Gospel of John (17.3). This is exactly the discovery expressed in Psalm 73. The supplicant sees God and discovers that he needs nothing more, that in his contact with God everything has been granted him, true life.

Joseph Cardinal Ratzinger
God Is Near Us, p. 139

We are personally responsible for the piece of God's Kingdom that we are ourselves. Only when Christ is the only standard of our actions, when we do what he did and reject what he rejected, when his love of God and of mankind shines forth irresistibly through us... only then is Christ present in these times and is born in us; only then can there be peace on earth around us.

Fr. Werenfried van Straaten

God does not enter into competition with earthly powers in this world. He does not marshal his divisions alongside other divisions. God did not send twelve legions of angels to assist Jesus in the Garden of Olives (cf. Mt 26.53). He contrasts the noisy and ostentatious power of this world with the defenceless power of love, which succumbs to death on the Cross and dies ever anew throughout history; yet it is this same love which constitutes the new divine intervention that opposes injustice and ushers in the kingdom of God. God is different – this is what they now come to realise. And it means that they themselves must now become different, they must learn God's ways.

Pope Benedict XVI
Homily at the vigil with the young people,
World Youth Day, Cologne, 24th August 2005

Because he has descended right to the depths of the earth (Eph 4.9 ff.), God is no longer merely a god up there, but God surrounds us from above, from below, and from within: he is all in all, and therefore all in all belongs to us: "All that is mine is yours." God's being "all in all" began with Christ's renunciation on the Cross of what was properly his. It will be complete when the son finally hands over to the father the kingdom, that is, ingathered humanity and the creation that is carried with them (1 Cor 15.28).

Joseph Cardinal Ratzinger
God Is Near Us, p. 144

Jesus is adjusting the ideas of the disciples to the fact that the Messiah is not appearing as the Saviour or the glorious powerful hero to restore the renown of Israel as a powerful state, as of old. He doesn't even call himself Messiah, but Son of Man. His way, quite to the contrary, lies in powerlessness and in suffering death, betrayed to the heathen, as he says, and brought by the heathen to the Cross. The disciples would have to learn that the kingdom of God comes into the world in that way, and in no other.

Joseph Cardinal Ratzinger
God and the World, p. 324

In the kingdom of the Father there are no things that "belong" to a person, no "shares" that one can demand as of right. For the love of God is not divisible, but gives itself completely. It is free, and sets us free. Love can only be received by those who trust in it, never by those who demand it.

Fr. Werenfried van Straaten

Earth becomes heaven, becomes the kingdom of God, whenever God's will is done there as in heaven… For the kingdom of God is *his* kingdom, not our kingdom, not within our sway; because it is so, it is final and can be relied upon. But it is always quite near wherever God's will is accepted. For that is where truth springs up, justice arises, love comes to be.

Joseph Cardinal Ratzinger
God Is Near Us, p. 143

151

The effect of the presence of the Lord upon everything within us that is interwoven with injustice, with hate, and with lies will be as a burning flame. It will become a purifying pain, which will burn away from within us everything that cannot be reconciled with eternity, with the living cycle of Christ's love.

Joseph Cardinal Ratzinger
God Is Near Us, p. 146

Neither war nor peace can ever cause the truth of Our Lord's words to waver. He is and remains the same for all eternity and his words will never pass away. And so our eternal happiness is inseparably bound up with Christ. Only together with him, the Head, can we, the members of his Mystical Body, become sharers in the kingdom of Heaven and in his glory.

Fr. Werenfried van Straaten

God's work... cannot be defended with the sword, as has unfortunately been attempted again and again. Anyone who wants to defend God by force is already by that very fact opposing him.

Joseph Cardinal Ratzinger
God and the World, p. 328

Disputes about faith will never end. The dispute is always at the same time a man's struggle with himself and a struggle with God, which will last until the end of history dawns.

Joseph Cardinal Ratzinger
God and the World, p. 33

Life shared with God, eternal life within temporal life, is possible because of God's living with us: Christ is God being here with us. In him has God time for us and thus at the same time the opening of time into eternity.

Joseph Cardinal Ratzinger
God Is Near Us, p. 144

Ecumenism

All the ends of the earth shall remember
and turn to the Lord; and all the families
of the nations shall worship before him.
(Psalm 22(21).27 RSV)

We seek an ecumenism of Christian solidarity! There must be no more competition, no more mistrust, no more xenophobia between two Churches that belong together.

Fr. Werenfried van Straaten

The unity of Christians cannot be restored by some kind of political coup or by cutting the Gordian knot with a sword. It's a matter of living processes. It's a matter of living processes. And neither a pope nor a World Council of Churches can simply say: 'Dear friends, let's do it this way!' Faith is something alive and deeply rooted in each one of us and is answerable to God. The Pope… has no totalitarian or absolute powers but is serving the obedience of faith.

Joseph Cardinal Ratzinger
God and the World, p. 453

True love does not eliminate legitimate differences, but harmonises them in a superior unity that is not ordered from the *outside* but gives form from *within,* so to speak, to the whole. As the mystery of communion unites man and woman in that community of love and life known as matrimony, it too forms the Church into a community of love, uniting a bountiful wealth of gifts and traditions.

Pope Benedict XVI
Homily at the conclusion of the Week of Prayer
for Christian Unity, 25th January 2006

May God grant us a quick arrival at the hoped-for full communion. The reformation of our unity will make evangelisation more effective. Unity is our common mission; it is the condition that enables the light of Christ to be spread better in every corner of the world, so that men and women convert and are saved. The road stretches before us! And yet, we must not lose trust; instead, with greater vigour we must once more continue our journey together. Christ walks before us and accompanies us. We count on his unfailing presence and humbly and tirelessly implore from him the precious gift of unity and peace.

Pope Benedict XVI
Homily at the conclusion of the Week of Prayer
for Christian Unity, 25th January 2006

Our divisions are the greatest threat to the kingdom of God. For Jesus remains in our midst only for as long as we are one in his name. Without him we can do nothing. That is why the prayer and last will of Jesus was for the unity of his disciples. It is the hallmark of all true Christians.

Fr. Werenfried van Straaten

More than ever I believe in my vocation to preach reconciliation, in season and out of season, to urge on the Church in the West to an active love for our Orthodox brethren, who suffered most under communism and are now the most endangered part of Christendom.

Fr. Werenfried van Straaten

The model of unity or oneness toward which one should strive is consequently not the indivisibility of the atom, the smallest unity, which cannot be divided up any further; the authentic acme of unity is the unity created by love. The multi-unity that grows in love is a more radical, truer unity than the unity of the 'atom'.

Joseph Cardinal Ratzinger
Introduction to Christianity, p. 179

The Lord Jesus, who broke down the "dividing wall of hostility" (Eph 2.14) with the blood of his Passion, will not fail to grant to those who faithfully invoke him the strength to heal every wound. But it is always necessary to start anew from this point: *"God is love."*

Pope Benedict XVI
Homily at the conclusion of the Week of Prayer
for Christian Unity, 25th January 2006

Our desire for reconciliation will only be credible if we approach the Russian people – who suffered more and longer than any other under the communist yoke – with hands full of love and generosity... Words are of no use here, only deeds! Not a single Russian will believe that we love him unless we are also ready to help him.

Fr. Werenfried van Straaten

Those who suppress devotion to Mary, practised since the beginning of Christendom in the Eastern and Western Church, not only break a sacred bond that still unites us to our Orthodox brethren, but in effect reject also the poor of the *Magnificat* and of the Sermon on the Mount, who are the true people of God.

Fr. Werenfried van Straaten

Sadly, there are many whose desire for peace springs from the love of a unity without substance – in other words, from the love of a lie. But we do not have the right to throw away the truth that Christ has entrusted to us, merely for the sake of a false notion of 'tolerance'. Sometimes we have the duty to be 'intolerant'.

Fr. Werenfried van Straaten

Humanity

What is man that you are mindful of him,
or the son of man, that you care for him?
(Hebrews 2.6 – cf. Psalm 8.5 NAB)

God is the first 'home' of human beings, and only by dwelling in God do men and women burn with a flame of divine love that can set the world 'aflame'.

Pope Benedict XVI
Message for World Mission Sunday,
29th April 2006

Each [person] requires the creative courage to live one's own life, and not just to turn oneself into a copy of someone else.

Joseph Cardinal Ratzinger
God and the World, p. 279

God alone can save us. That is a shock to our pride and humiliating for humanity. But it is not frightening. God is the only ally who is without self-interest. His salvation is different from every human way out, but at the same time surer, more lasting and infinitely better.

Fr. Werenfried van Straaten

The communion of Saints consists not only of the great men and women who went before us and whose names we know. All of us belong to the communion of Saints.

Pope Benedict XVI
Mass for the inauguration of the pontificate,
24th April 2005

The human race – every one of us – is the sheep lost in the desert which no longer knows the way. The son of God will not let this happen; he cannot abandon humanity in so wretched a condition. He leaps to his feet and abandons the glory of heaven, in order to go in search of the sheep and pursue it, all the way to the Cross. He takes it upon his shoulders and carries our humanity; he carries us all – he is the good shepherd who lays down his life for the sheep.

Pope Benedict XVI
Mass for the inauguration of the pontificate,
24th April 2005

All people desire to leave a lasting mark. But what endures? Money does not. Even buildings do not, nor books. After a certain time, longer or shorter, all these things disappear. The only thing that lasts for ever is the human soul, the human person created by God for eternity.

Pope Benedict XVI
Mass Pro Elegendo Pontefice, 18th April 2005

Christ is the prototype of man. We cannot see in him the image of God in his eternal infinity, but we can see the image in which he chose to portray himself. From that point, we are no longer making an image, but God himself has shown us an image. Here he looks at us and speaks to us.

Joseph Cardinal Ratzinger
God and the World, p. 24

God's love does not differentiate between the newly conceived infant still in his or her mother's womb and the child or young person, or the adult and the elderly person. God does not distinguish between them because he sees an impression of his own image and likeness (Gn 1. 26) in each one. He makes no distinctions because he perceives in all of them a reflection of the face of his only-begotten son, whom "he chose... before the foundation of the world... He destined us in love to be his sons... according to the purpose of his will." (Eph 1.4-6)

Pope Benedict XVI
Address to the General Assembly of the Pontifical Academy for Life, 27th February 2006

Whenever God is not there, the human being is no longer respected either. Only if God's splendour shines on the human face is the human image of God protected by a dignity which subsequently no one must violate.

Pope Benedict XVI
Pastoral visit to the parish of St Anne at the Vatican, 5th February 2006

Although the Lord is risen from the grave to return to his Father, he nevertheless wishes to remain on earth in a new humanity – our humanity – in order to multiply his love, to draw all men to himself and to be present in his world in a million different shapes and forms.

Fr. Werenfried van Straaten

The Saints and the Blesseds did not doggedly seek their own happiness, but simply wanted to give themselves, because the light of Christ had shone upon them. They show us the way to attain happiness, they show us how to be truly human.

Pope Benedict XVI
Homily at the vigil with the young people, World Youth Day, Cologne, 24th August 2005

God is not a remote God, too distant or too great to be bothered with our trifles. Since God is great, he can also be concerned with small things. Since he is great, the soul of man, the same man, created through eternal love, is not a small thing but great, and worthy of God's love.

Pope Benedict XVI
Mass of the Lord's Supper, Holy Thursday, 13th April 2006

During the first half of this century I saw for myself the consequences of two world wars. The material damage was immeasurable, the loss of human life irreplaceable. But worse still was the destruction in the hearts and souls of men. For something had been lost there that was infinitely more precious than the towns and monuments – even than the human life. For the greatest damage of these wars was surely the loss of the Spirit of Christ and of those Christ-like features that make man like God and give him the right to call him "Father".

Fr. Werenfried van Straaten

Christ did not promise an easy life. Those who desire comforts have dialled the wrong number. Rather, he shows us the way to great things, the good, towards an authentic human life.

Pope Benedict XVI
To the German-speaking pilgrims on the day after the official start of his pontificate, 25th April 2005

It was never the wish of the Church to conform Christian life to the spirit of the world. Every genuine reform has meant a return to the spirit of Christ. As John the Baptist put it: "He must grow greater, I must grow less." (Jn 3.30) When God is put down and man exalted there can be no reform, but only decay.

Fr. Werenfried van Straaten

If... the essential characteristic of man is his likeness to God, his capacity for love, then humanity as a whole and each of us individually can only survive where there is love and where we are taught the way to this love. We come back to Christ: the saving act of Christ consists of making comprehensible to us the fact that God loves us... He brings this home to each of us, and by his way of the Cross he accompanies each of us along the path of losing ourselves. And by transforming the law of love into the gift of love, he overcomes that greatest loneliness of all, the state of being unredeemed.

Joseph Cardinal Ratzinger
God and the World, p. 190

We are called to live as brothers and sisters of Jesus, to feel that we are sons and daughters of the same Father. This is a gift that overturns every purely human idea and plan.

Pope Benedict XVI
To the 43rd World Day of Prayer for
Spiritual Vocations, 7th May 2006

In today's world, where certain erroneous concepts concerning the human being, freedom and love are spreading, we must never tire of presenting anew the truth about the family institution, as God has desired it since creation.

Pope Benedict XVI
To the Plenary Assembly of the Pontifical
Council for the Family, 13th May 2006

The purpose of our lives is to reveal God to men. And only where God is seen does life truly begin. Only when we meet the living God in Christ do we know what life is. We are not some casual and meaningless product of evolution. Each of us is the result of a thought of God. Each of us is willed, each of us is loved, each of us is necessary. There is nothing more beautiful than to be surprised by the Gospel, by the encounter with Christ. There is nothing more beautiful than to know him and to speak to others of our friendship with him.

Pope Benedict XVI
Address to mark the official beginning
of his pontificate, 24th April 2005

Weaknesses and human limitations do not present an obstacle, as long as they help make us more aware of the fact that we are in need of the redeeming grace of Christ. This is the experience of St Paul who confessed: "I will all the more gladly boast of my weaknesses, that the power of Christ may rest upon me." (2 Cor 12.9)

Pope Benedict XVI
To the 43rd World Day of Prayer for
Spiritual Vocations, 7th May 2006

If we let Christ into our lives, we lose nothing, nothing, absolutely nothing of what makes life free, beautiful and great. No! Only in this friendship are the doors of life opened wide. Only in this friendship is the great potential of human existence truly revealed. Only in this friendship do we experience beauty and liberation.

Pope Benedict XVI
Address to mark the official beginning
of his pontificate, 24th April 2005

If it is true that at the end stands the triumph of spirit, that is, the triumph of truth, freedom, and love, then it is not some force or other that finally ends up victorious; what stands at the end is a countenance. The omega of the world is a 'you', a person, an individual... Man, the person, always takes precedence over the mere idea.

Joseph Cardinal Ratzinger
Introduction to Christianity, p. 322

Do not be afraid of Christ! He takes nothing away, and he gives you everything. When we give ourselves to him, we receive a hundredfold in return. Yes, open, open wide the doors to Christ – and you will find true life.

Pope Benedict XVI
Address to mark the official beginning
of his pontificate, 24th Apri 20051

Just as God can only come to man through other human beings, so men can only come to one another through God. The relationship with God is not the private sphere of each individual, into which no one else can or may enter. Rather it is entirely private and entirely public at the same time... Only together can men come to God; the very search for God directs them towards one another.

Joseph Cardinal Ratzinger
Faith and the Future

Man has within him the breath of God. He is capable of relating to God; he can pass beyond material creation. He is unique. He stands in the sight of God and is in a special sense directed toward God. There is indeed a new breath within him, the divine factor that has been introduced into creation. It is most important to see this special creation by God in order to perceive the uniqueness and value of man and, thereby, the basis of all human rights.

Joseph Cardinal Ratzinger
God and the World, p. 77

It must be forcefully stated that the human being cannot and must not ever be sacrificed to the success of science and technology: this is why the so-called "anthropological question" assumes its full importance. For us, the heirs of the humanist tradition founded on Christian values, this question should be faced in the light of the inspiring principles of our civilisation, which found in European universities authentic laboratories for research and for deepening knowledge.

Pope Benedict XVI

To the participants in the seminar organised by the Congregation for Catholic Education, 1st April 2006

Judaism, Christianity and Islam believe in the one God, creator of heaven and earth. It follows, therefore, that all three monotheistic religions are called to cooperate with one another for the common good of humanity, serving the cause of justice and peace in the world. This is especially important today when particular attention must be given to teaching respect for God, for religions and their symbols, and for holy sites and places of worship. Religious leaders have a responsibility to work for reconciliation through genuine dialogue and acts of human solidarity.

Pope Benedict XVI

Address to the members of the American Jewish Committee, 16th March 2006

In nature it is a matter of growing and dying. In Christ, however, we can see that man is an end in himself. He is not just one element in the great process of growing-and-dying, but is, and remains, a separate end product of creation. In that way he has been plucked up out of the mere turbulence of the eternal rise-and-decline and has been brought within the unending and creative love of God.

Joseph Cardinal Ratzinger
God and the World, p. 97

As human beings we are there so that God can come to people by way of other people. He always comes to people through people. So we too always come to him through other people who are being led by him, in whom he himself meets us and opens us up to him. If we could lift ourselves up to the ultimate degree simply by reading Holy Scriptures, then this would be just another philosophical movement, without this element of community that is such a vital element in faith.

Joseph Cardinal Ratzinger
God and the World, p. 70

God has not divided history into a light half and a dark one. He has not divided people into those who are redeemed and those he has forgotten. There is only one, indivisible history, and it is characterised as a whole by the weakness and wretchedness of man, and as a whole it stands beneath the merciful love of God, who constantly surrounds and supports this history.

Pope Benedict XVI
What it means to be a Christian, p. 35

Today man would like to have total, sole and absolute dominion over his time. We have in fact forgotten how important it is to allow God into our time and not merely to use time as an element made available for our own private purposes. It is a matter of standing aside from concepts of what is useful or practical – and thereby becoming available for others and for ourselves.

Joseph Cardinal Ratzinger
God and the World, p. 171

Church

For I am the least of the apostles,
unfit to be called an apostle,
because I persecuted the church of God.
(1 Corinthians 15.9 RSV)

There is much that could be criticised in the Church. We know this and the Lord himself told us so: it is a net with good fish and bad fish, a field with wheat and darnel. Pope John Paul II, as well as revealing the true face of the Church in the many Saints that he canonised, also asked pardon for the wrong that was done in the course of history through the words and deeds of members of the Church.

Pope Benedict XVI

Homily at the vigil with the young people,
World Youth Day, Cologne, 24th August 2005

I do not have to carry alone what in truth I could never carry alone. All the Saints of God are there to protect me, to sustain me and to carry me. And your prayers, my dear friends, your indulgence, your love, your faith and your hope accompany me. Indeed, the Communion of Saints consists not only of the great men and women who went before us and whose names we know. All of us belong to the Communion of Saints, we who have been baptised in the name of the Father, and of the Son and of the Holy Spirit, we who draw life from the gift of Christ's Body and Blood, through which he transforms us and makes us like himself.

Pope Benedict XVI

Address to mark the official beginning
of his pontificate, 24th April 2005

The destruction of authority in the Church, that guarantee of its unity and driving force of its love, seem to be a liberation to some people, but it is, as St. Peter writes, often merely a hypocritical pretext for vice. This need of the Church also requires an answer from us.

Fr. Werenfried van Straaten

The Church is alive and we are seeing it: we are experiencing the joy that the Risen Lord promised his followers. The Church is alive – she is alive because Christ is alive, because he is truly risen.

Pope Benedict XVI
Address to mark the official beginning
of his pontificate, 24th April 2005

The Pope knows that in his important decisions, he is bound to the great community of faith of all times, to the binding interpretations that have developed throughout the Church's pilgrimage. Thus, his power is not being above, but at the service of, the Word of God. It is incumbent upon him to ensure that this Word continues to be present in its greatness and to resound in its purity, so that it is not torn to pieces by continuous changes in usage.

Pope Benedict XVI
Mass and Installation in the Chair of the Bishop
of Rome, Lateran Basilica, 7th May 2005

The power that Christ conferred upon Peter and his successors is, in an absolute sense, a mandate to serve. The power of teaching in the Church involves a commitment to the service of obedience to the faith.

Pope Benedict XVI
Mass and Installation in the Chair of the Bishop
of Rome, Lateran Basilica, 7th May 2005

Within the Church, one will above all have to look at whether someone is only proclaiming himself, trying to force his own personal views upon me. Or whether he has the humility to put himself at the service of the faith of the Church and become a servant of the common Word, the only Word.

Joseph Cardinal Ratzinger
God and the World, p. 290

It is actually consoling to realise that there is darnel in the Church. In this way, despite all our defects, we can still hope to be counted among the disciples of Jesus, who came to call sinners. The Church is like a human family, but at the same time it is also the great family of God, through which he establishes an overarching communion and unity that embraces every continent, culture and nation. So we are glad to belong to this great family... In this great band of pilgrims we walk side by side with Christ... the star that enlightens our history.

Pope Benedict XVI
Homily at the vigil with the young people,
World Youth Day, Cologne, 24th August 2005

The school of faith is not a triumphal march but a journey marked daily by suffering and love, trials and faithfulness. Peter, who promised absolute fidelity, knew the bitterness and humiliation of denial: the arrogant man learns the costly lesson of humility. Peter, too, must learn that he is weak and in need of forgiveness.

Pope Benedict XVI
General audience, 24th May 2006

You know I am a priest and that my work for the Church in need, which is receiving your support, must therefore be of a priestly nature; that is our task, therefore, not to save bodies in the first place but souls; that we must not in the first place endeavour to reorganise economic life but the life of Christ in the hearts of the people.

Fr. Werenfried van Straaten

"You are Christ!"
"You are Peter!"
I seem to be reliving the same Gospel scene; I, the successor of Peter, repeat with trepidation the anxious words of the fisherman of Galilee and listen once again with deep emotion to the reassuring promise of the divine master. Although the weight of responsibility laid on my own poor shoulders is enormous, there is no doubt that the divine power on which I can count is boundless.

Pope Benedict XVI
First homily as Pope, 20th April 2005

Peter, too, must learn that he is weak and in need of forgiveness. Once his attitude changes and he understands the truth of his weak heart of a believing sinner, he weeps in a fit of liberating repentance. After this weeping he is finally ready for his mission.

Pope Benedict XVI
General audience, 24th May 2006

Christ is the constant power that gives life to this vine and makes it capable of bearing fruit. In this sense the reality of the Church is far greater than what you can tabulate in statistics or achieve by decisions. This reality is a living organism, whose life cycle derives from Christ himself.

Joseph Cardinal Ratzinger
God and the World, p. 343

We believe that the Church is holy, but that there are sinners among her members. We need to reject the desire to identify only with those who are sinless. How could the Church have excluded sinners from her ranks? It is for their salvation that Jesus took flesh, died and rose again. We must therefore learn to live Christian penance with sincerity.

Pope Benedict XVI
Meeting with the clergy in the Cathedral
of St John, Warsaw, Poland, 25th May 2006

The faithful expect only one thing from priests: that they be specialists in promoting the encounter between man and God. The priest is not asked to be an expert in economics, construction or politics. He is expected to be an expert in the spiritual life.

Pope Benedict XVI
Meeting with the clergy in the Cathedral
of St John, Warsaw, Poland, 25th May 2006

In the face of the temptations of relativism or the permissive society, there is absolutely no need for the priest to know all the latest, changing currents of thought; what the faithful expect from him is that he be a witness to the eternal wisdom contained in the revealed word.

Pope Benedict XVI
Meeting with the clergy in the Cathedral
of St John, Warsaw, Poland, 25th May 2006

Without the Holy Spirit, the Church would be reduced to merely a human organisation, weighed down by its own structures. But, for its part, in the plans of God, the Spirit habitually makes use of human mediations to act in history.

Pope Benedict XVI
Regina Caeli *message, 15th May 2005*

The task of the shepherd, the task of the fisher of men, can often seem wearisome. But it is beautiful and wonderful, because it is truly a service to joy, to God's joy which longs to break into the world.

Pope Benedict XVI
Address to mark the official beginning
of his pontificate, 24th April 2005

In the mystery of the Church, the mystical Body of Christ, the divine power of love changes the heart of man, making him able to communicate the love of God to his brothers and sisters. Throughout the centuries many men and women, transformed by divine love, have consecrated their lives to the cause of the Kingdom. Already on the shores of the Sea of Galilee, many allowed themselves to be won by Jesus: they were in search of healing in body or spirit, and they were touched by the power of his grace. Others were chosen personally by him and became his apostles. We also find some, like Mary Magdalene and others, who followed him on their own initiative, simply out of love. Like the disciple John, they too found a special place in his heart.

Pope Benedict XVI
To the 43rd World Day of Prayer
for Spiritual Vocations, 7th May 2006

The Church is holy, even if her members need to be purified, in order that holiness, which is a gift of God, can shine forth from them with its full splendour.

Pope Benedict XVI
To the 43rd World Day of Prayer
for Spiritual Vocations, 7th May 2006

Feeding the Lord's flock, therefore, is a ministry of vigilant love that demands our total dedication, to the last drop of energy and, if necessary, the sacrifice of our lives.

Pope Benedict XVI
To the members of the 11th ordinary council of the General
Secretariat of the Synod of Bishops,
1st June 2006

Today too the Church and the successors of the apostles are told to put out into the deep sea of history and to let down the nets, so as to win men and women over to the Gospel – to God, to Christ, to true life.

Pope Benedict XVI
Address to mark the official beginning
of his pontificate, 24th April 2005

Persecution

Blessed are those who are persecuted
for righteousness' sake,
for theirs is the kingdom of heaven.
(Matthew 5.8 RSV)

You cannot have any part in Christ's peace if you leave the suffering Christ to his fate and do nothing for him who calls for help in millions of the persecuted.

Fr. Werenfried van Straaten

The secret heroism of persecuted Christians, the patience of the sick, the agony of the dying, the solitude of the abandoned – all suffering accepted in love and all temptation overcome, each victory over cowardice and selfishness and every prayer of the hundreds of thousands who fly to the protection of Mary – in short, everything, at some time and in some place resounds to the benefit of the suffering Church in our days.

Fr. Werenfried van Straaten

Christianity is being tested. Persecuted Christians are being tested in their faith. They ought to have a blind trust in God and believe in his unfathomable providence. But we are all being tested in our love. We have to prove that we possess love, in spite of all our differences of opinion… a love that is patient, a love that understands, a love that helps and comforts, a love that burns like a flame in the dark night of the persecuted Church and sets hope burning there, so that they do not fall into despair in their affliction.

Fr. Werenfried van Straaten

The teaching of Christ, the joyful, fascinating message of love was not written down by him. In the first centuries of the Church, when the martyrs were shedding their blood and the survivors were seeking refuge in the catacombs, it was not learned from books. It was proclaimed by the radiant lives and the glad deaths of a handful of true Christians. Never has the Church conquered a pagan world so swiftly as in those days.

Fr. Werenfried van Straaten

Even in those lands where God's enemies have burnt every copy of Holy Scripture, this Gospel can still be clearly read in the lives and behaviour of Christians in whom the all-merciful God is again made manifest.

Fr. Werenfried van Straaten

An 'anti-God' power has declared war on eternal Love and is trying to quench the fire that God's son brought to earth and wants to see burning. On the day that this fire blazes up in our hearts and in the world, there will be no more communism; then all men of good will – even though atheists – will acknowledge God in our love.

Fr. Werenfried van Straaten

As long as suffering is merely described in words, or measured in figures, it can be passed over. But, made incarnate in real people with individual names and faces, who form a living reproach, it creates unrest.

Fr. Werenfried van Straaten

Think, when adoring the Sacred Heart of Jesus, not only of the Lord who suffers and bleeds for the sins of the world, but also of all the persecuted who suffer and bleed with him for us. Not only do they share in his humiliation and misery, but from their mouths we also hear his bitter lament: "I looked for someone to pity me but there was no one; I sought for one who would comfort me but I found none..."

Fr. Werenfried van Straaten

During Passiontide in the churches, the crosses are veiled, but at the same time, throughout the wide world, they are being used to torture and to kill – crosses on which our brothers are dying. And in these brothers Christ is dying...

Fr. Werenfried van Straaten

We are no better than the rest and yet we are better off. We, the small minority who for the most part still live in ease, have to tread a quite different path to Heaven from the great majority, who perish today amid poverty and fear, bloodshed and tears. Are we on the right path?

Fr. Werenfried van Straaten

Never and nowhere will the Church be destroyed – as long as her priests give a clear and irresistible witness to a life that can be lived only through Christ and in God's strength.

Fr. Werenfried van Straaten

When, today, we look at past history, then we have to say that it is not the Church of those popes who were universal monarchs; the Church of those leaders who knew how to get on well with the world. Rather, what strengthens our faith, what remains constant, what gives us hope, is the Church of the suffering. She stands, to the present day, as a sign that God exists and that man is not just a cesspit, but that he can be saved. This is true of the martyrs of the first three centuries, and then right up to Maximilian Kolbe and the many unnamed witnesses who gave their lives for the Lord under the dictatorships of our own day; whether they had to die for their faith or whether they had to let themselves be trampled on, day after day and year after year, for his sake.

Joseph Cardinal Ratzinger
God Is Near Us, p. 40

Let us share both in the sorrow and the gladness of the persecuted Church so that pain may be divided and joy doubled and this dark would become a little easier to live in.

Fr. Werenfried van Straaten

The tyrants who take God's place can only maintain their power by illegal, heartless, immoral, unsocial and inhuman means. An irrefutable proof of this is given to us by communism. It has banished God and called in the devil.

Fr. Werenfried van Straaten

If we really love this forsaken Christ, who is crucified anew, we may not deny the cross in our own lives. For no one can be united to him unless he shares in his sufferings.

Fr. Werenfried van Straaten

Although I have already seen a great deal of distress I have never got used to it. Every time I see it again it grips me in the depth of my being. Indelibly the memory of it is printed in my mind. It never leaves me and its presence demands every day a fresh answer.

Fr. Werenfried van Straaten

Never has so much been said about the Church of the poor as in our days, but never have the poor, the humble, the unlettered, the children – to all of whom the kingdom of Heaven was promised – felt so abandoned.

Fr. Werenfried van Straaten

Much that causes you fear should in fact give you courage. For in God's plan even the devil has a task to fulfil. The hour of Satan's fury is also the hour of your purification. True, those who are purified like gold in the crucible have to suffer greatly, but Christ says: "Blessed are those who mourn; blessed are those who hunger and thirst; blessed are those who suffer persecution, for theirs is the kingdom of Heaven."

Fr. Werenfried van Straaten

The suffering of the martyrs is for the good of everyone. Therefore it is a high privilege to be allowed to suffer mockery for Jesus' sake, to be united with the suffering Christ and to have a part in his work of redemption.

Fr. Werenfried van Straaten

The first Christians were filled with respect for their brethren who suffered persecution for Christ's sake. The martyrs were the very first to be honoured as saints. The Eucharist was celebrated on their graves to express and strengthen our spiritual union with the sacrifice of their lives. In these days there is little to be felt of this union.

Fr. Werenfried van Straaten

Should we not we troubled by the gruesome fact that millions of people must live through the darkest hours of their lives without experiencing the love of God, because millions of others, who could make this love of God a tangible reality for them, instead remain hard-hearted and indifferent?

Fr. Werenfried van Straaten

Jesus stands for all victims of brute force: in the twentieth century itself we have seen again how inventive human cruelty can be; how cruelty in the act of destroying the image of man in others, dishonours and destroys that image in itself.

Joseph Cardinal Ratzinger
God and the World, p. 333

We personally share the blame for this outrage if we do not do everything we can to help to eliminate it… *everything* we can.

Fr. Werenfried van Straaten

Why are we so well off? These afflicted people live under the same sun and under the same stars as we do. On the sixth day God also created them to become lords of creation. Where is their kingship?

Fr. Werenfried van Straaten

More than any others the persecuted Christians have a right to our love. It is our duty to be more and more conscious of our solidarity with them. This can also help us not to overestimate the artificially magnified problems of the post-conciliar Church.

Fr. Werenfried van Straaten

We cannot and we may not remove the Cross from a world that is yearning for redemption; there is therefore nothing else for us to do but to help our Lord, who suffers in his afflicted brethren, to carry his Cross.

Fr. Werenfried van Straaten

Secularism

For the time is coming when people will not endure
sound teaching, but having itching ears they will
accumulate for themselves teachers to suit their own
likings, and will turn away from listening to the truth
and wander into myths.
(2 Timothy 4. 3-4 RSV)

Look around in this world. See how terribly cold and dark it has become. For God, who is light and fire, is gone from the United Nations, from the parliaments, from international conferences, from politics, from legislation, from education, from morals, from many sermons, from the hearts of millions of men. God is gone. But his absence bears eloquent witness; it declares insistently that we cannot live without him. It is the irrefutable proof that he is the One who is indispensable and utterly necessary, without whom life has no meaning.

Fr. Werenfried van Straaten

Whenever we try to do without God, try to bypass him and to put the world right by our own systems, whenever we think that the satisfaction of material needs is the real key to the problem, then we solve nothing; we destroy things; we do the work of Satan.

Joseph Cardinal Ratzinger
God and the World, p. 254

It is not ideologies that save the world, but only a return to the living God, our Creator, the guarantor of our freedom, the guarantor of what is really good and true.

Pope Benedict XVI
Homily at the vigil with the young people
World Youth Day, Cologne, 24th August 2005

In the end, the claim that just social structures would make works of charity superfluous masks a materialist conception of man: the mistaken notion that man can live "by bread alone" (Mt 4.4; Vgl. Dn 8.3) a conviction that demeans man and ultimately disregards all that is specifically human.

Pope Benedict XVI
Deus Caritas Est, 28

Wherever a person or a society refuses to take God's business seriously, in some way or other the fate of Gomorrah overtakes them again. When any society turns away from fellowship with the living God, it cuts the inner roots of its social organism.

Joseph Cardinal Ratzinger
God and the World, p. 237

Each single misuse of God's name, each and every act that obscures his face so that he can no longer be recognised, leaves behind it a monstrous track of filth. The great power of atheism, the rejection of God, and indifference to God are quite inexplicable without this repeated misuse of God's name. His face was disfigured to such an extent that man felt bound to turn away from it. It has in this way long since become clear what terrible effects the breach of this commandment can have in human history.

Joseph Cardinal Ratzinger
God and the World, p. 220

You can never predict in advance how things will turn out. Anyone who is extrapolating the decline of the Church in academic, statistical fashion from the situation in Europe is failing to recognise the unpredictable nature of human history in general – and in particular, God's power to take the initiative by intervening, as he is always able to do.

Joseph Cardinal Ratzinger
God and the World, p. 458

To see God's banishment there is no need to turn to the communist world. In our own midst, in the name of a liberal or socialist humanitarianism, the son of the living God, with his passionate love for the heavenly Father and for immortal souls, with his law of the Cross, with his inescapable demand of obedience, humility, chastity, self-denial and poverty, is being banished from press, radio and television, from preaching and catechism, from marriage and education, from churches and tabernacles.

Fr. Werenfried van Straaten

There is a lot of talk today about 'the pilgrim people'. In actual fact, seldom before has Christianity so tried to establish itself firmly on this earth. It banished heaven from consciousness and places all its hope in a happiness that expects from this world only, notwithstanding the preacher's devastating judgement: "Vanity of vanities, all is vanity!"

Fr. Werenfried van Straaten

Only from the Saints, only from God does true revolution come, the definitive way to change the world. In the last century we experienced revolutions with a common programme – expecting nothing more from God, they assumed total responsibility for the cause of the world in order to change it. And this, as we saw, meant that a human and partial point of view was always taken as an absolute guiding principle. Absolutising what is not absolute but relative is called totalitarianism. It does not liberate man, but takes away his dignity and enslaves him.

Pope Benedict XVI
Homily at the vigil with the young people
World Youth Day, Cologne, 24th August 2005

True revolution consists in simply turning to God who is the measure of what is right and who at the same time is everlasting love. And what could ever save us apart from love?

Pope Benedict XVI
Homily at the vigil with the young people
World Youth Day, Cologne, 24th August 2005

Acknowledgements

Our grateful thanks to:

Ignatius Press for permission to reproduce quotations from the following works by Pope Benedict XVI:
Faith and the Future
God and the World
God is Near Us
Introduction to Christianity
What it Means to be a Christian
All rights reserved, Ignatius Press.

Libreria Editrice Vaticana for permission to reproduce all other quotations from Pope Benedict XVI

All quotations from Fr Werenfried van Straaten
Copyright © 2007 Aid to the Church in Need

Index of quotations from Pope Benedict XVI

Addresses

1st June 2006: To the members of the 11th ordinary council of the General Secretariat of the Synod of Bishops
pp. 58, 184

Clergy

15th May 2005: Priestly ordination in St Peter's
pp. 17, 28, 41, 45, 47, 144

10th February 2006: To the participants of the Plenary Assembly of the Congregation for the Doctrine of the Faith
p. 126

18th February 2006: To the permanent deacons of the diocese of Rome
p. 127

25th May 2006: Meeting with the clergy in the Cathedral of St John, Warsaw, Poland
pp. 68, 181, 182, 182

Encyclicals

Deus Caritas Est
pp. 31, 44, 66, 77, 107, 108, 110, 111, 113, 114, 114, 115, 116, 121, 124, 126, 126, 129, 129, 198

General Audiences

Mass

5th February 2006: Pastoral visit to the parish of St Anne at the Vatican
pp. 145, 165

Publications

Faith and the Future
pp. 44, 73, 76, 78, 82, 84, 95, 170

God and the World
pp. 12, 13, 17, 18, 23, 32, 33, 35, 39, 40, 42, 43, 44, 47, 49, 63, 63, 65, 74, 82, 83, 84, 85, 88, 90, 95, 96, 108, 109, 109, 110, 112, 113, 113, 118, 121, 151, 152, 152, 157, 163, 164, 167, 170, 172, 172, 173, 179, 181, 192, 197, 198, 198, 199

God is Near Us
pp. 69, 78, 135, 136, 136, 137, 138, 138, 149, 150, 151, 152, 153, 190

Introduction to Christianity
pp. 42, 43, 44, 73, 80, 96, 107, 115, 159, 169

What it means to be a Christian
pp. 11, 47, 57, 89, 101, 102, 105, 106, 107, 118, 173

World Youth Day 2005, Cologne, Germany

18th August 2005: Papal welcoming ceremony on the banks of the Rhine
p. 20

Aid to the Church in Need

Aid to the Church in Need supports the faithful wherever they are persecuted, oppressed or in pastoral need. ACN is a Catholic charity, helping to bring Christ to the world.

ACN was founded on Christmas Day 1947 by Father Werenfried van Straaten and is now a universal pastoral charity of the Catholic Church, with thousands of projects all over the world:

- Seminarians are trained
- Bibles and religious literature are printed
- Priests and religious are supported
- Refugees are helped
- Churches and chapels are built and restored
- Over 43 million of ACN's Child's Bibles have been printed in more than 150 languages
- Religious programmes are broadcast

For regular updates from the suffering Church around the world, and to view our full range of books, cards, gifts and music, please log on to **www.acnuk.org**

Aid to the Church in Need

In the UK

12-14 Benhill Avenue
Sutton
SM1 4DA

Tel: 020 8642 8668
Email: acn@acnuk.org
www.acnuk.org

In Australia

PO Box 6245
Blacktown DC
NSW 2148

Tel: +61 (0) 2 9679 1929
Email: info@aidtochurch.org
www.aidtochurch.org

In Canada

PO Box 670, STN H
Montreal
QC H3G 2M6

Tel: +1 (1) 800 585 6333
Email: info@acn-aed-ca.org
www.acn-aed-ca.org

In Ireland

151 St Mobhi Road
Glasnevin
Dublin 9

Tel: +353 (0) 1 83 77 516
Email: churchinneed@eircom.net
www.acnirl.org

In the USA

725 Leonard Street
PO Box 220384
Brooklyn
NY 11222-0384

Tel: +1 (1) 800 628 6333
Email: info@acnusa.org
www.churchinneed.com